The Silent Film Quarterly

Volume 1, Issue I
Fall 2015

Second Edition

Edited by Charles Epting

The Silent Film Quarterly

Volume I, Issue 1
Fall 2015

Table of Contents

Classic Features:

Interviews:

Editor's Message

Welcome to the inaugural issue of *The Silent Film Quarterly*!

The idea for *Silent Film Quarterly* stemmed from a personal desire to write articles about silent films. As there was no such outlet for me, I began to contemplate the feasibility of a magazine solely devoted to the silent era. There are a large number of silent film blogs and websites in existence, as well as several extremely active Facebook groups—which told me that the interest was there. Several phone calls to fellow historians assured me that there was a wealth of content just waiting to be written. The pieces began falling into place perfectly.

One conscious decision I made from the very beginning was to focus on lesser-known silent films. There are about a dozen silent films that seem to receive a majority of people's attention—films like *Metropolis* and *Sunrise* and *It* and *Intolerance*. When most people think of Keaton, Chaplin, and Lloyd—the "big three"—they invariably think of *The General*, *City Lights*, and *Safety Last!*, respectively. But these three have so many incredible films between them that often go unnoticed—not to mention the work of other comedians like Max Linder and Harry Langdon.

With that in mind, I want this magazine to help pay tribute to the unsung heroes of the silent era, as well as the forgotten films of the era's biggest stars. Obviously this is made more difficult by the large number of lost silent films, but are still many more films in existence than most people realize.

Much of the inspiration for *Silent Film Quarterly* also came from countless hours of poring over silent era movie magazines. *Photoplay*, *Motion Picture*, and *Screenland* all influenced the layout and content of this magazine, and I like to think of *Silent Film Quarterly* as something of a spiritual successor to those magazines that documented the silent era firsthand.

Each issue of *Silent Film Quarterly* will include a number of departments in addition to the features that will comprise the bulk of the magazine:

"Silent Star In Brief" is a brief biography of a forgotten silent film star—looking at actors like Wanda Hawley and Charles Clary instead of Mary Pickford and Buster Keaton. Focus will be placed on actors and actresses whose filmographies are largely lost, as their legacies are most often neglected.

"In Their Own Words" is a collection of original material from the silent era—facts and figures from movie magazines, articles written by and about Hollywood's biggest stars, and other firsthand sources that have not been republished in nearly a century. This issue, for example, features Lillian Gish advocating Liberty bonds during the Great War, Colleen Moore musing on the inevitability of bobbed hair, and more.

"Celluloid Collectibles" will feature a write-up of an artifact from or about the silent film era, often one that is widely available and affordable for collectors today. While items such as posters and autographs can be prohibitively rare in many cases, there are still opportunities to own a piece of this era of cinema history.

"Silents in Review" features reviews of silent films—both shorts and feature length movies—of all genres. The focus will be on lesser-known films (especially those that are not commercially available), in order to provide readers with valuable content. Reviews of *It* and *City Lights* are a dime a dozen; the same cannot be said of Colleen Moore's *Orchids and Ermine* (featured in this issue).

The main body of the magazine will consist of feature-length articles and interviews. The features will often be a mixture of vintage articles penned by or about silent film stars, as well as original content written exclusively for *Silent Film Quarterly*. Interviews will always be exclusive to the magazine, and will feature an eclectic mix of everyone from preservationists and historians to modern actors and relatives of silent film stars.

In this first issue, I am thrilled to have articles contributed by some incredible researchers and writers. Annette D'Agostino Lloyd, renowned for her biographical work on Harold Lloyd, has contributed an original article on *Moving Picture World* magazine. E.J. Stephens—author of numerous books about Los Angeles's early film studios—has written about silver screen cowboy William S. Hart, and science fiction-aficionado Cory Gross details 1925's legendary blockbuster *The Lost World*. It is my hope that these articles are not just enjoyable to read, but inspire future research and writing in the world of silent films.

Blogs and Facebook groups are fantastic ways to share information about the silent film era, but there is still something inherently special about holding a print magazine in your hands. There is a permanence—a timelessness—that a print magazine has that is different from online means of communication. Movie magazines have been around since the earliest days of cinema; at the time, they were the only way for fans to get more information about their favorite stars and pictures. Today the world is obviously very different—but the role of the movie magazine remains unchanged, bringing fans closer to the matinee idols on the silver screen.

Thank you for taking the time to read this magazine. With your support and a little bit of luck, it is my hope that it will continue to grow and develop. Silent films have played an incredibly important role in my life, as I know they have for many others. May this magazine serve as a tribute to that era.

Charles Epting
Los Angeles, California
2015

About the Editor:

Charles Epting is a recent graduate of the University of Southern California and the author of four books. His first, *University Park, Los Angeles: A Brief History*, recounts the history of USC from its formation in 1880 through the present day, focusing specifically on the cultural impact the school has had on Los Angeles and the nation.

His next two books, *The New Deal in Orange County* and *Orange County Pioneers: Oral Histories from the Works Progress Administration*, document the impact of President Franklin Roosevelt's New Deal programs in Orange County, California; because of his New Deal writings, Epting is also a research associate for UC Berkeley's Living New Deal program. His most recent book, *Victorian Los Angeles*, was published in March of 2015. In addition to his books, Epting has written articles for *The American Philatelist*, *Missouri Life*, *Idaho Magazine*, and *The Santa Monica Mirror*, amongst other publications.

Charles Epting's newest project is a biography of silent film star Bebe Daniels, which will be published in the spring of 2016 by McFarland Books.

Write for Silent Film Quarterly!

Want to write for *Silent Film Quarterly*? The magazine is always looking for interesting original content about the silent era, including feature articles and reviews of silent films. Please contact the editor at charleseptingauthor@gmail.com if interested or for more information.

In Their Own Words
Short primary sources from the silent era
· · ·

500 Newspaper Critics Pick Ten Most Beautiful Actresses
From Photoplay, December 1925

1. Corinne Griffith
2. Mary Astor
3. Alice Terry
4. Florence Vidor
5. May McAvoy
6. Norma Shearer
7. Gloria Swanson
8. May Allison
9. Marion Davies
10. Pola Negri

Living Your Character
By William S. Hart
From Motion Picture, April 1917

"Putting over" a lead character on the screen requires thought and common-sense. This sounds like a truism—I mean common-sense in forgetting one's studied technique and carriage and simply dressing and feeling the part.

"Live the character, if it is a true one," is my motto, and forget everything else. Think as he would think, and you'll do what he would do. If a story demands that I assume the role of a minister, then, thruout six or seven weeks that are filled with producing the story, I try to forget that William S. Hart is just a plain actor, and try to think, study and live as a Right Reverend would. Then I am governed by what my inner judgment tells me the character would do under the conditions prescribed by the author's scenario.

If the role is that of a bad man, all my feelings are those of a desperate character thruout the play. And so it goes in all my parts, which, for the most part, are of a Western nature. When the picture is complete I relax and become myself again.

This state of pleasant, personal freedom generally lasts about four or five days, until the study of a new story begins by Doctor Jekylling myself into a new character.

It is strange, when you take up the character of another, how you can enter into the emotions and feelings of the role. As an illustration, in taking a scene in "The Patriot," some time ago, I was called upon to weep hysterically over the grave of my dead son. His death had occurred while I was away from home, and, as a result, I was turning traitor to my country. Subconsciously I knew that I was kneeling by a mound of earth and that no one was buried there, least of all any child of mine; but the emotional qualities of the character so worked on my imagination that it was easy to play the scene. I was tortured with hate, and grief, and self-pity, and with the thought that I was turning my back on my country. I just naturally turned loose and cried.

When an actor feels the character that he is playing, the "close-up" is an invaluable asset. If it is a tense scene, where the character is under great mental stress and his facial mobility is such that he can put over that emotion to his audience, then, despite all rules of technique to the contrary, I claim that the scene demands a "close-up" of the actor's face cut quickly into the main scene. The "close-up" is often used, unfortunately, when unnecessary, when it only serves to distract the attention of the audience from the principal scene, but it is really the only medium by which an actor can accurately register a particular emotion.

I want all my "sets" just as accurately made as possible, as this gives the atmosphere and is a material assistance in feeling the part. I make up extemporaneous lines for myself and for the rest of those in the cast, always striving to maintain the author's original intent and atmosphere. It is remarkable how a few lines help; they drown out the whir of the camera, and one can speak as the character would speak under the same circumstances, thereby joining the last dividing link between himself and the part. I do not believe in useless dialog, which is unintelligible on the screen and likewise distracting, but a few snappy lines here and there, particularly in moments of crisis and climax, are certainly very much in order.

Tricks are not my forte. I spoke of using common-sense, and this is one of the places that applies. The public always spots any little, theatrical and stagey tricks a lead character "pulls" for the purpose of riveting attention on himself. True characterizations do not need tricks to push them thru. Perhaps I had better explain what I mean by tricks: little, cute things, not necessarily funny, but done at a moment when another player is rightfully entitled to the attention of the audience and "pulled" for the purpose of turning that attention on himself.

Some actors hold to the belief that if they are contracted to play leads they must appear in nine-tenths of the scenes. I believe that the lead character is not necessarily the one to receive the most footage. The leading character naturally enjoys the center of interest, but let the footage take care of itself. I prefer about forty per cent, of the total footage, provided the part gives me an acting role. By "acting role" I mean the part that I can feel and play in such a manner that it is vital.

I think the most disagreeable part that I ever had was in "The Aryan," It was hard for me to really feel it, being that of a white man who, forswearing his race, makes outlaw Mexicans his comrades and allows white women to be attacked by them. It is difficult to put all one's decent instincts aside and live and think as such a despicable character must have done. But by allowing myself to think only of the terrible wrong that the white race had done me—pure imagery—I settled into it, and I am sure Bessie Love at the time believed I was the typical brute.

I suppose every actor has his own ideas on how certain roles should be played. I try for true understanding and naturalness and leave the rest to the cameraman. And I find that I am seldom called upon to re-enact a scene for want of color. I am not a person who permits enthusiasm to run away with my better judgment, and I do not think I over-feel a part. The public, of course, must judge my efforts.

Ten Best Films of 1925
From New York Times, January 10, 1926

1. The Big Parade
2. The Last Laugh
3. The Unholy Three
4. The Gold Rush
5. The Merry Widow
6. The Dark Angel
7. Don Q, Son of Zorro
8. Ben-Hur
9. Stella Dallas
10. A Kiss for Cinderella

Short Skirts and Bobbed Hair Are Here to Stay Forever
By Colleen Moore
From New York Herald-Tribune, September 6, 1925

Don't worry, girls. No edict of fashion arbiters will ever swathe you again in long and cumbersome skirts, or make unfashionable your bobbed hair. Women have declared an independence of style dictators in these respects. My recent trip to European centers has convinced me of this. Long skirts, corsets and flowing tresses have gone; at least, for those who do no twant them.

The American girl will see to this. She is independent, a thinker. She will not follow slavishly the ordinances of those who, in the past, have decreed this or that for her to wear. The old-fashioned girl, with the curls and long skirts, the corset and tight bodice gowns that draped down and about the floor, will not be seen again—except on the walls suspended by a wire and encased in a gilded frame.

She has gone forever. Why? Simply because the girls are advancing in thought and in so doing have realized these modes are out of date—entirely so.

The girls of to-day and to-morrow will rebel against a dictator. They will no longer permit any single person or any group of persons dictating what they shall and shall not accept in style. They have made their own styles and nothing in the world will prevent their being carried out. This has been proved very decidedly.

Bobbed hair was scorned when it first appeared in America. Yet bobbed hair is, in my opinion, here to stay. Why? Because it is easy to keep neat and quicker to dress. Time is essence in this day and age.

Short skirts have found favor with our American girls. Years before they were considered crude and bold. The wearer was looked upon with serious consideration. But short skirts are here. They are in Paris, London, too. America has accepted them despite rulings from fashion experts that they will be lowered. The American girl will not permit them being lowered. Why? Because they are comfortable as they are. They aid a girl's grace in walking, and they are not dust collectors.

What American girl of to-day advocates the corset? Very few. Corsets have gone. The store shelves contain dusty boxes in which repose the tight-fitting pieces of harness that once caught the fancy of all the shoppers. Corsets will never come back. The modern girl has had a taste of freedom from their tightness. She has gained a point. They are useless and uncomfortable, no matter how beautiful and how much lace and silk trimmings they possess.

Simplicity in dress is the slogan that the girl of to-morrow will blast forth upon the fashion dictators. They must conform with the general feeling of American womanhood. Frills and laces and ribbons are no longer sought after. The plain gown, short-skirted, corsetless figure is what the typical girl in Los Angeles, New York and Squeedunk will accept—nothing else!

In days gone by a certain group of fashion experts would band together and advocate certain styles for each season. No more. It is not what one, two or a hundred designers wish, but it is what the great mass —the hundreds of thousands of girls in this land want—comfort, grace, simplicity.

Why Every One Should Buy Liberty Bonds
By Lillian Gish
From Chicago Daily Tribune, October 8, 1918

I know 500,000,000 reasons for buying a Liberty bond and not one against buying a bond. Certainly every life in this country and in the lands of our allies offers a reason, for each of us considers his or her life and freedom worth any protection necessary even unto death.

No matter how pressed for funds, one would lend a friend a few dollars in the time of greatest need, knowing the money would be returned with interest. And how much greater is one's duty to one's country than even to one's dearest friends?

If you had been with me in London one afternoon a "four-minute" man of a different breed than ours would have given you so many reasons for buying bonds that you would never think of reasons again but just give and give and give. He was a Hun aviator and he was over London, just four minutes. And he dropped bombs.

One dropped on a public school where little children were at their studies. It was a big school. Nearly all of the children were killed or maimed. Their mothers came when the alarm was spread. They fought with the police. Most of the mothers had husbands at war. Their faces and their outcries! How much those women had given!

A few liberty bonds measure up very small compared with a little child, or a brother, or father, or sister, or husband.

In the prayer hook of democracy today the fly-leaf should be a Liberty bold.

Have you yours?

Ideal Cast Contest Winners
From Motion Picture, February 1922

As voted on by *Motion Picture* magazine's readers:

Leading Woman: Norma Talmadge
Leading Man: Wallace Reid
Villain: Lew Cody
Vampire: Bebe Daniels
Character Man: Theodore Roberts
Character Woman: Vera Gordon
Comedian: Harold Lloyd
Comedienne: Dorothy Gish
Child: Jackie Coogan
Director: D.W. Griffith

Scriptural Appeal Given by Arbuckle
By Roscoe "Fatty" Arbuckle
From various papers, December 25, 1922

All I ask is the rights of an American citizen—American fair play. Through misfortune and tragic incident, I was tried on a charge of which I was absolutely innocent. A jury composed of eight men and four women, all of whom were of high character and excellent civic standing, and all of whom were members of churches of various faiths, found me innocent. Not only that but the same jury sent a message to the American people in this language:

"Acquittal is not enough for Roscoe Arbuckle. We feel that a great injustice has been done him. We also feel that it was only our plain duty to give him this exoneration under the evidence, for there was not the slightest proof adduced to connect him in any way with the commission of a crime."

Unlike the jury, those denouncing me heard no part of the evidence and are without knowledge of the facts. The scripture says that 'as ye judge, so shall ye be judged.' How would my accusers like to be judged as they are judging me?

The institutions of my country, the courts and juries, and the law of the land, have declared me innocent, and I am entitled to the benefit and protection of the law. Those who are unjustly, untruthfully, maliciously and venomously attacking me are refusing to abide by the established law of the land.

I am not only wholly innocent, but more than that. There is a higher law which deals with the spiritual side of mankind, and surely this Christmas time should not be the season when the voice of the Pharisee is heard in the land.

But even suppose that I had not been able to establish my innocence, but that I were conscientiously endeavoring through an orderly life to atone for my mistakes, would I not be entitled to an appeal for forgiveness, according to the scriptures, the letter of which so many in the pulpit seem to observe, and the spirit of which some in the pulpit seem to ignore?

It is not difficult to visualize at this time of the year, which commemorates the birth of Christ, what might have happened if some of those who now heartlessly denounce me had been present when the savior forgave the penitent thief on the cross in words that have influenced the human race more than any other words ever uttered. Would not some of those persons have denounced and stoned him for what he said?

No one ever saw a picture of mine that was not clean and wholesome. No one ever will see such a picture. I claim the right of work and service.

The sentiment of every church on Christmas day will be 'peace on earth and good will to all mankind.' What will be the attitude the day after Christmas to me?"

All articles are reproduced exactly as they originally appeared.

Silents in Review

· · ·

A Trip To Paramountown (1922)

Length: *two reels (10 minutes, 26 seconds surviving)*

Release date: *July 10, 1922*

Cast: *Dorothy Dalton (on the set of* Fool's Paradise, Moran of the Lady Letty, The Woman Who Walked Alone, *and* The Siren Call); *Penrhyn Stanlaws (dir.) and Anna Q. Nilsson (on the set of* Pink Gods); *William DeMille (dir.), William Boyd, Conrad Nagel, Wallace Reid, Bebe Daniels, and Julia Faye (on the set of* Nice People); *Fred Niblo (dir.), Rudolph Valentino, Walter Long, Lila Lee, and Nita Naldi (on the set of* Blood and Sand); *Sam Wood (dir.), Gloria Swanson, Harrison Ford, and Walter Hiers (on the set of* Her Gilded Cage); *Cecil B. DeMille (dir.), Jeanie MacPherson (writ.), Thomas Meighan, Leatrice Joy, George Fawcett, Lois Wilson (on the set of* Manslaughter); *George Fitzmaurice (dir.), Ben Lyon, and Billie Dove (on the set of* The Tender Hour)*

· · ·

1923's *Hollywood* is one of the most sought-after lost silent films, primarily due to its cameos from dozens of Hollywood's biggest stars (including Chaplin, Pickford, Fairbanks, and a destitute Arbuckle). Much less well-known, however, is its predecessor *A Trip to Paramountown*, made in 1922 to highlight many of Paramount's forthcoming productions.

A Trip to Paramountown is often listed as a two-reeler, and the fact that the surviving print is only 10 minutes and 26 seconds suggests that an entire reel may be missing. However, what survives is a fascinating glimpse at some of the studio's biggest stars and directors.

Highlights include footage of Cecil B. DeMille and screenwriter mistress Jeanie MacPherson behind the scenes on the set of *Manslaughter*, Valentino appearing in full toreador costume on the set of *Blood and Sand*, and Sam Wood finding a lounging Swanson unprepared for the day's shoot.

Special effects gags are used to a fault. Wallace Reid picks up a toy car featuring a miniature Wallace Reid behind the wheel, while Bebe Daniels plays with a dancing Bebe Daniels doll (through the camera magic of a split-screen). It seems as if Paramount was simply trying to demonstrate their technical capabilities to impress prospective moviegoers. However, the unnecessary effects are redeemed by the rarity of footage of Reid less than a year before his death.

It is curious that George Fitzmaurice's 1927 production *The Tender Hour* is included in the short, as the movie post-dates the other Paramount productions by five years. As the title cards are not labeled "*A Trip to Paramountown*," it seems most likely that segment (and perhaps Anna Q. Nilsson's closing scene) are from a later promotional film.

A Trip to Paramountown is hard to judge on its own merits, as the enjoyment in watching the short lies primarily in the fact that some of 1922's biggest stars are shown in natural, candid environments. For fans of Swanson and Valentino, it is a must. For casual silent film fans, it is simply a mishmash of unrelated scenes from vastly different productions. In short: more appealing from a historical stand point than an aesthetic one.

-Charles Epting

A Trip to Paramountown *is available as part of Flicker Alley's collection,* "Valentino: Rediscovering an Icon of Silent Film"

Orchids and Ermine (1927)

Length: *6,734 feet, six reels (62 minutes)*

Release date: *March 6, 1927*

Cast: *Colleen Moore as "Pink" Watson, Jack Mulhall as Richard Tabor, Sam Hardy as Hank, Gwen Lee as Ermintrude, Alma Bennett as the Vamp*

· · ·

A FIRST NATIONAL PICTURE

JOHN McCORMICK presents

COLLEEN

MOORE

ORCHIDS and ERMINE

With . . . . . JACK MULHALL
Story and Scenario by CAREY WILSON
An ALFRED SANTELL
production

'Pink' Watson hooked me about three minutes into *Orchids and Ermine*. It was the scene where she wraps a white cat around her neck like a mink stole. This is a woman who has nothing, but knows exactly what she wants.

Why 'orchids and ermine'? Because they're both are items of luxury—two of many (along with the stole) that Pink plans to be swathed in once she marries rich. Step one, then, is finding a rich man to marry. For Pink (Colleen Moore), this will mean goodbye to her receptionist job at the cement factory, where everything and everyone, including Pink and the men she meets, are covered in dust.

Rich people prefer the city, so Pink will find a job there. She'll work at a luxury hotel, right out in the lobby, where a cutie like herself will be easy to spot. And she'll operate the switchboard. Then everyone's business will have to go through her.

Is Pink a gold-digger? I don't think so. Money isn't all that matters to her. She's simply a woman confident enough in her self-worth to demand the best, and while she has little money of her own, minimal social position and average looks, she's also too smart and determined to be denied.

Just compare her to her best friend, Ermintrude. If Pink's best weapon is her wits, Ermintrude (Gwen Lee) is unarmed. She is the hotel flower girl and (implicit) tramp, viewing marriage as her first and last step to easy living. She also gauges a man's wealth by how much he spends, and so throws herself at the most ostentatious cads she can find. This is bad strategy. Her dates are more like deals, and the men want payment upfront.

Not that we should judge, of course. The desire both women have to marry well makes them no different from thousands of other people populating the silent screen, and the realms of theatre, literature and legend for centuries before that. None of them said they were marrying for money, but the ones they won over were always well-off. Even Cinderella had it both ways, and you couldn't blame her for being pleased about it. Pink differs from Ermintrude, and all the rest, only in her self-reliance. Yes, she wants a man's money, but she'll determine exactly how he gives it to her.

Seems like I'm writing more about Pink than the movie she's in. That's because *Orchids and Ermine* is such a clear star-vehicle for the popular Moore, who's in nearly every scene. Any number of actresses could have played Pink, but none could've done it with more snap than Colleen Moore. She imbues Pink with a rascally charm that makes her lovable no matter what she does.

The story surrounding her can be summed up quickly. Pink's hotel is visited by the youthful, bookish Richard Tabor, whose fames precedes him thanks to a windfall in the oil market. Tabor (Jack Mulhall) is anything but a playboy, yet he's deluged by one starstruck femme after the next, all eyeing his huge bank account. Tabor's so weary of the chase that he devises a plan to switch places with his driver, Hank (Sam Hardy), a man who's happy to take control of Tabor's blank cheques and unsought attention. Pink falls victim to the millionaire's ruse, but the whole thing becomes more of a problem for Tabor than for her. It is Tabor, not Pink, who ends up giving chase, protesting that indeed, he is who he says he is now, not who he said he was the day before—and all to win the hand of a woman who's supposedly trying to land a rich man at any cost.

It's all quite fun—just insubstantial. The direction is fine too, and the supporting cast is able to a man, but *Orchids and Ermine* remains strictly a formula comedy, in service of its star.

That's about all I've got for *Orchids and Ermine*, except this: I wish it was a talkie. The film has waves of Jazz-Age one-liners, most of them delivered by Moore, and her banter translates into dozens of intertitles. Too many. Pink had a lot to say, and even two years later, that mouth would have roared, and roared loud.

-Chris Edwards
originally published on Silent Volume
http://silent-volume.blogspot.com

Orchids and Ermine *was formerly available on DVD from Grapevine Video*

Why Change Your Wife? (1920)
Length: *7,613 feet, eight reels (91 minutes)*
Release date: *May 2, 1920*
Cast: *Thomas Meighan as Robert Gordon, Gloria Swanson as Beth Gordon, Bebe Daniels as Sally Clark, Theodore Kosloff as Radinoff*

• • •

Upon watching *Why Change Your Wife?*, it is not immediately apparent that it is a Cecil B. DeMille film. One of his domestic "marriage films," as they are commonly known, the movie clearly lacks the budget or ambition of DeMille's biblical epics (such as *The Ten Commandments*). Despite this, it is nevertheless a simple and charming take on married life—although at times *Why Change Your Wife?* relies too heavily on the star power of its two leading ladies.

Why Change Your Wife? was something of a spiritual successor to 1919's *Don't Change Your Husband*, which also featured Gloria Swanson but otherwise had an entirely different cast. The film tells the story of Robert Gordon (Thomas Meighan), a disgruntled husband with a dowdy wife who cannot avoid the affections of shop girl Sally Clark (Bebe Daniels). Thinking that Sally would be an improvement over Beth (Swanson), he takes up a relationship with her—only to find an entirely new slew of domestic problems.

Eventually, Robert finds himself at a resort with both of his lovers. A slip on a banana peel (perhaps the film's weakest plot device) renders Gordon immobilized, and the film's climax consists of a catfight between Beth and Sally that ends in the former fending off her husband's seductress. A reformed, liberal Beth then rekindles her marriage—in no small part due to her now-revealing clothes and jazzy taste in music. Sally, on the other hand, takes up a new relationship with a foreign violin player.

The moral of the film is clearly stated in its final intertitle: "And now you know what every husband knows: that a man would rather have his wife for his sweetheart than any other woman: but Ladies: if you would be your husband's sweetheart, you simply must learn when to forget that you're his wife." Such a message may seem tame today, but it was undoubtedly progressive for 1920 (and reviews by more traditional critics ascertain its provocative nature).

With such a risque closing thought, it should come as no surprise that a huge selling point for the film was the appearance of Swanson and Daniels in several revealing costumes. Swanson was, at the time, one of the screen's leading sex symbols, and her presence all but guaranteed the film would be at least a moderate success.

Bebe Daniels, on the other hand, was relatively unknown as a dramatic actress. Beloved by the masses as Harold Lloyd's leading lady for years, *Why Change Your Wife?* is arguably her first humanizing performance (both *Male and Female* and *Everywoman*, which predate *Why Change Your Wife?*, have her playing only minor roles with no character development). Sally Clark is somewhat of a complex character —appearing flirtatious and charming at first, but revealing her true colors when she declares, "There's only one good thing about marriage anyway—and that's alimony."

Why Change Your Wife? is a decent film to watch for those unfamiliar with the breadth of DeMille's work. Meighan's performance is ultimately forgettable and Swanson has much better films. Interestingly it is the newcomer Bebe Daniels who steals the film, but even her vampish role cannot save the film as a whole.

-Charles Epting

Why Change Your Wife? *is available on DVD from Image Entertainment or for streaming online at* archive.org

Mr. Wu (1927)

Length: *7,603 feet, eight reels (90 minutes)*
Release date: *March 26, 1927*
Cast: *Lon Chaney as Mr. Wu and Mr. Wu's grandfather, Louise Dresser as Mrs. Gregory, Renée Adorée as Nang Ping, Anna May Wong as Loo Song*

• • •

In 1927, Lon Chaney returned to his makeup mastery the year after *The Blackbird*. In *Mr. Wu*, he again played two roles: Mr. Wu and Grandfather Wu. Also starring Renee Adoree as Mr. Wu's first daughter (Wu Nang Ping) and Anna May Wong as his second daughter (Loo Song), the film is based on a stage play written by Harold Owen and Harry M. Vernon. Matheson Lang, who portrayed Mr. Wu in the 1913 West End production, actually appeared in the first film version of this story in 1919. The plot starts out with little Wu, whose grandfather entrusts his education to an English associate. After Wu is married off to a delicate girl who dies giving birth to his daughter, he swears to raise the child as a daughter and a son. He arranges a marriage for Nang Ping to a mandarin when she comes of age, but instead she falls in love with a young Englishman Basil Gregory. When Basil breaks the news that he must return to Britain with his family, Nang Ping tells him that she carries his child, then confesses that she was merely testing to see if he was an "honorable man." A nosy gardener reveals the relationship to Mr. Wu who is enraged and becomes resolved to follow his culture's ancient law by killing his dishonored daughter and exacting revenge on Basil and his family.

In viewing this film today, one must keep in mind the limited opportunities there were for Asian actors in early Hollywood. Often, major stars like Chaney and Adoree were called upon to don "yellowface" while actual Asian players were relegated to the more minor roles and those of extras. Anna May Wong, who was Chinese-American and quite prolific in silent films, could have easily pulled off the role of Nang Ping, but directors were still resistant to this idea in the 1920s. The other issue was that many U.S. states still had anti-miscegenation laws on the books preventing racially mixed marriages until they were ruled unconstitutional in 1967, which made many studios squeamish about depicting mixed relationships on film in the early days. Seeing genuine Asian actors alongside non-Asians in makeup may be disturbing to some today, but it does demonstrate how far we've come as a society in terms of entertainment over the last 100 years.

-Mark Ambrose

Mr. Wu *is available on DVD from Warner Bros.*

Celluloid Collectibles

Artifacts from and about the silent era

. . .

In 1991, famed caricaturist Al Hirschfeld was commissioned to create a series of five postage stamps for the United States Postal Service depicting famous American comedians. The stamps proved so popular that three years later Hirschfeld once again was chosen to design a series of postage stamps—this time depicting "Stars of the Silent Screen."

Ten performers were chosen to be part of the 29¢ stamp issue: Rudolph Valentino, Clara Bow, Charlie Chaplin, Lon Chaney, John Gilbert, ZaSu Pitts, Harold Lloyd, the Keystone Cops, Theda Bara, and Buster Keaton. The stamps were dedicated on April 27, 1994, in conjunction with the 37th annual San Francisco International Film Festival. Buster Keaton's *The Goat* and Harold Lloyd's *Safety Last!* were screened at the ceremony.

With only ten stamps in the series, there are bound to be major exclusions. Notably absent are Mary Pickford and Douglas Fairbanks (the latter of whom was featured on a stamp in 1984) and the Gish Sisters, all of whom played a pivotal role in the early years of Hollywood. However, given the limited scope of the series the performers chosen do a good job at representing the breadth of silent cinema.

Hirschfeld's trademark line-drawings depict the essence of each actor and actress perfectly—from Keaton's deadpan expression to Chaplin's ill-fitting trousers, every portrait is unmistakable. Despite a USPS rule against hidden messages in postage stamps, Hirschfeld was allowed to include his trademark NINA's in both the comedian and silent film stamps.

Original Hirschfeld artwork can be prohibitively expensive, but his series of postage stamps serves as an affordable means of owning some of his characteristic designs. A complete set of the ten stamps in mint condition sells for little more than face value today, and can be had for approximately $5 on eBay (a set of first day covers for the entire series is slightly more expensive, starting at around $12).

For the serious silent film fan, 1994's "Stars of the Silent Screen" stamps are an absolute must.

Silent Star In Brief
Mary Miles Minter
• • •

In 1921, Mary Miles Minter was one of the most famous names on the planet. Just a few years later, she would be an pariah in Hollywood, foregoing her fame and stardom in favor of self-imposed exile. Because of this she remains all but forgotten, one of cinema's leading starlets ruined by scandal.

Mary Miles Minter was born Juliet Reilly on born April 25, 1902, in Shreveport, Louisiana. She began her stage career at the age of five, and made her film debut only five years later in a one-reeler called *The Nurse*. Reilly adopted her new alliterative name as part of a ploy devised by her mother to avoid child labor laws; once in Hollywood, Mary Miles Minter stuck for the rest of her career.

As an ingenue Minter was often compared to the equally-demure Mary

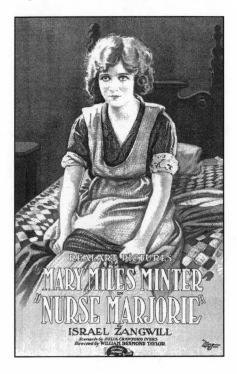

Pickford, whom she rivaled in popularity at her peak. In June of 1919, Adolph Zukor shocked the world when he signed Mary Miles Minter to a $1.3 million contract for his new production company, Realart Pictures. At the time, it was the largest contract in the history of Hollywood.

Her superstardom would prove to be short-lived, as in 1922 Minter became embroiled in one of Hollywood's first major scandals. On February 1, 1922, director William Desmond Taylor was found murdered in his home; amongst his possessions were coded love letters written by the young actress. Minter was 19 at the time of his death—Taylor was 49. Today, many historians believe that her love may not have been reciprocated by her director; at the time, even a tenuous connection was enough to prove a fatal blow to her career. To make matters worse Minter's mother, Broadway actress Charlotte Shelby, was amongst the leading suspects in the murder case.

After starring in her final film role (1923's *The Trail of the Lonesome Pine*) Mary Miles Minter lived out the rest of her life in relative anonymity. She claimed she did not regret losing her Hollywood career, and at the time of her death in 1984 few people realized just how popular she had once been. When she suffered her fatal stroke, the *Los Angeles Times* ran a headline that simply read, "Mary Minter, a Golden Girl Tinged With Scandal, Dies." Of her 54 films only about a dozen survive today, partially explaining her obscurity.

Mary Miles Minter was an early casualty of Hollywood; ultimately innocent, her involvement with the industry's dangerous underbelly ultimately cost her her career. Unfortunately, it is now impossible for modern audiences to accurately judge her creative output.

Recommended Films:
Nurse Marjorie (1920)
The Eyes of Julia Deep (1918)

Vol. 6., No. 4.   January 29, 1910   Price, 10 Cents

Published Weekly by THE WORLD PHOTOGRAPHIC PUBLISHING CO., 125 E. 23d ST., NEW YORK

The Moving Picture World:
Where Everything Old Is New Again

by Annette D'Agostino Lloyd

Movie magazines are an invaluable resource to silent film scholars and fans alike. Join noted author and researcher Annette D'Agostino Lloyd as she describes the fascinating story of one of the most important such publications.

• • •

Chances are, if you are reading this, you are a dedicated silent film student and/or chronicler. And if that is the case, chances are even greater that you have, at one time or another, benefitted from the insights preserved within the pages of the granddaddy of all film magazines, *The Moving Picture World*. If you haven't…well, I'm here to make your work a lot easier.

I first met this marvelous trade journal in 1993, while working on my first academic tome on Harold Lloyd. I needed reviews of Lloyd's earliest films, dating back to 1913, many of which are not available for me to personally assess. I decided to peruse all of the magazines of the day, and found MPW to be the best of them. So entranced was I of this lovely little journal that I decided, after finishing the Lloyd book, to compile two indexes to assist researchers in using *MPW*. More on that later.

First published on March 9, 1907, and remaining in circulation until December 31, 1927, *The Moving Picture World* offered 1084 issues, and 108,798 pages of information which, now, *is* film history. The 89 volumes averaged 1222 pages per volume, and each issue averaged 100 pages. Based in New York, the *MPW* had a Spanish-language sister publication, *Cine Mundial*, and, over its nearly 21-year run, boasted the highest circulation of all similar periodicals. It merged with one of its competitors, *Exhibitors Herald*, in 1928.

The idea for a magazine called "The Moving Picture World" came, in a small office at 361 Broadway, New York, to James Petrie Chalmers, Jr., editor of the photographic publication *Camera and Dark Room*, and Alfred H. Saunders, editor of *Views and Film Index*, more commonly known as *The Film Index*. The first issue cost five cents, and contained sixteen pages, with three and a half pages devoted to advertising. The cover of Volume 1, Number 1 introduced the concept: "The Moving Picture World and View Photographer: The Only Independent Weekly Journal Published in the Interests of Manufacturers and Operators of Animated Photographs and Cinematograph Projection, Illustrated Songs, Lantern Lectures and Lantern Slide Makers." The March 9, 1907 editorial article explained the mission of this new paper: "It is our intention to give the best, and only the best, news concerning the film industry, describing briefly each new film as it is produced, taking note of its quality, and giving an unbiased opinion of its merits or demerits." Twelve thousand copies of the first issue were printed. They were all gone in a week.

The Moving Picture World was founded by J.P. Chalmers who, in the words of John Chalmers (later President of the Chalmers Publishing Company, distributor of *MPW* since 1912), "was privileged to lay the foundation of character and the high principles of independence, service, fair play and rugged honesty from which, we who have followed, have never departed." J.P. Chalmers led the publication until his untimely death at age 46, on March 27, 1912. He was attending a film convention at Dayton, Ohio, and his death resulted from a tragic fall down an elevator shaft: he thought he was entering a film projection booth, which similarly had sliding doors.

In June 1911, *The Moving Picture World* acquired *The Film Index*, which had been founded by William T. Rock of the Vitagraph Company and Jacques A. Berst of Pathe Freres. Originally a house organ (or, a magazine which listed the releases of a particular company), in 1909, when the Motion Picture Patents Company was formed, *The Film Index* became the organ of this company. Absorption of the *Index* by the *MPW* was a significant step in cinema history. While *The Moving Picture World* laid claim to being the first actual motion picture trade paper in America, it then merged with the first paper devoted to the films themselves. The focus became the trade *and* the films.

The various covers of *The Moving Picture World* reflect this. After a most bland initial series of covers, with stark advertising their hallmark, the trademark double pillar cover debuted on September 2, 1911. At first, the ornamental frame held a still from a film. As this was not particularly profitable, the cover, clearly the most valuable advertising position in the paper, resumed being devoted to trade advertisements for the remaining 16 years of its run, even as the basic cover formats changed. As ever, the emphasis was on the films and the companies making them—never did a player portrait appear on the cover, unless in an advertisement for a film.

The articles found in *The Moving Picture World* are markedly different from the typical "fan" magazine, for the simple reason that the periodical was not aimed at the film fan, but rather the theatre owner or the exhibitor who showed the films. The articles have an almost business-like frankness, simplicity and pointedness, and exhibitors relied on it for data which, more often than not, would be used in the publicity, or "exploitation," of a company, film, or star. There was little to no "fluff," and for that reason the journal came to be depended upon as a reliable and trustworthy source of factual and believable information on those persons, industries, films or innovations that were covered. Within the pages of *The Moving Picture World* are data that, perhaps, can be found nowhere else—dates of marriages, places of death, film debuts, honors, etc.

In the two *MPW* indexes that I published, I tried (and hopefully succeeded) to make *MPW* more accessible and easier to work with. My first book indexed the "un-indexed" years of 1907-1915 (starting in 1916, the year-end issues contained a sketchy, but still helpful, index of the year's articles). My second *MPW* index took two years to compile: I read each issue, and listed all articles on "filmmakers," which included before- and behind-the-camera personnel who actively made the films (I did not index the exhibitor-related articles). Both of my *MPW* books were books I needed while doing the first Lloyd book—I have been blessed to refer to my own books on *MPW* while doing subsequent research on all things Lloyd. I've been gratified to hear from many fellow researchers who told me that my books have made their work easier. That was my goal.

The Moving Picture World was the first trade magazine to use the airplane in the reporting of events in the industry; the first paper to carry a "radio photograph" sent from overseas, and the first publication to mail its product via the flat envelope method, "...far superior to the ordinary, cheaper, 'roll 'em-crease 'em' way."

In the March 11, 1922 issue of *The Moving Picture World*, the "Fifteenth Anniversary Number," several notable film luminaries offered statements of praise to the journal: "vigorous," "just," "a credit to the industry," "honest," "unbiased," "fearless"—sentiments indicative of the silent film industry's feelings about, and dependence upon, *The Moving Picture World*.

In the "Twentieth Anniversary Number" of The Moving Picture World, dated March 26, 1927, A.J. Chalmers, of the Chalmers Publishing Company, reported a brief history of the magazine in his article, "The Story of Twenty Years":

Two decades have gone by. Twenty years of motion picture history—all of them years characterized by hectic activity.... Throughout this span of time Moving Picture World has endeavored to serve a great art-industry honestly, fairly, and to the best of its ability. It has consistently maintained and protected its right as an independent publication to present its own editorial views.

On December 31, 1927, page 7, an announcement was released by John F. Chalmers: "With this issue *Moving Picture World* concludes publication as an individual trade paper and becomes merged with *Exhibitors Herald*. The combined publications will be published under the joint title, *Exhibitors Herald and Moving Picture World.*" Thus ended a nearly 21-year run, with 89 volumes accrued, and 1084 issues published.

In summing up attempts to copy the services provided by *The Moving Picture World*, Chalmers concluded, "They have all lacked the all important 'know how' and complete familiarity with the subject which so easily distinguishes a winner from an 'also ran.'" The researcher of today can still depend on *The Moving Picture World* for hard information, particularly in light of the film preservation movement, and the exciting rediscovery of thought-to-be-lost classics.

Ready to dig in and discover my favorite silent film trade journal? Here's how: visit mediahistoryproject.org/collections, where (so far) the marvelous team of dedicated professionals at the Media History Digital Library has scanned each issue from 1907-1919, with plans for more. (I wish they had been around when I was building my indexes; I used microfilm and hard copies, along with pencils and index cards!!!) Never before has it been easier to use and enjoy *The Moving Picture World*, where, truly, everything old IS new again!

Annette D'Agostino Lloyd is the foremost biographer of Harold Lloyd and one of the leading authorities on silent cinema. Her numerous works include her two aforementioned indices of Moving Picture World, *as well as* The Harold Lloyd Encyclopedia.

Moving Picture World Through the Years...

The first issue of *MPW*, March 9, 1907.

Moving Picture World Through the Years...

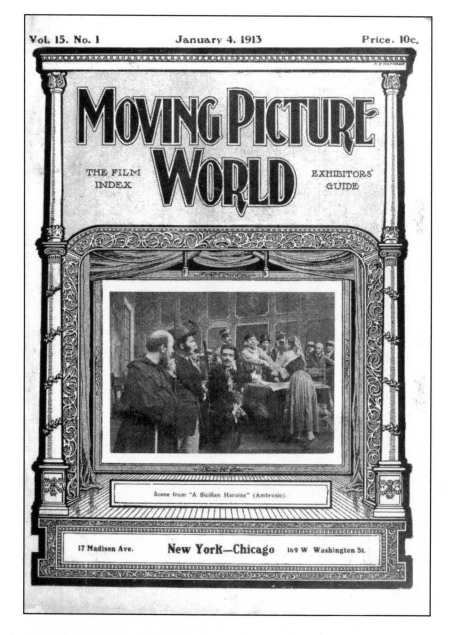

January 4, 1913 issue of *MPW.* On the cover is the Italian three-reeler, *A Sicilian Heroine.*

Moving Picture World **Through the Years...**

January 4, 1919 issue of *MPW.* At the time a subscription was $3 annually.

Moving Picture World Through the Years...

Robert Harron in *Coincidence* on the cover of the May 14, 1921 issue of
MPW.

Moving Picture World **Through the Years...**

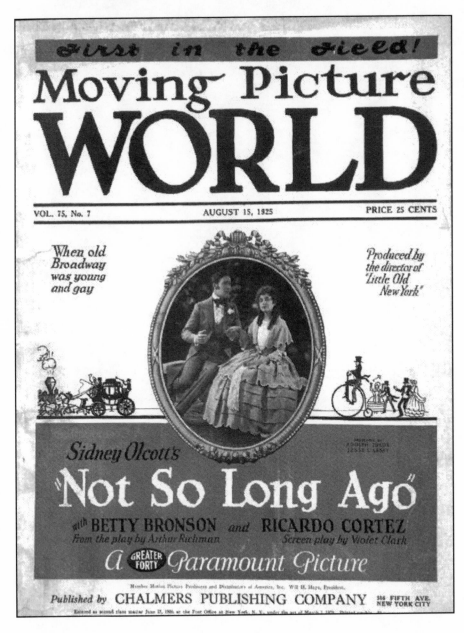

MPW's August 15, 1925 issue, featuring Betty Bronson and Ricardo Cortez
on the cover.

When Silents Roared:
Dinosaurs Take the Big Screen
by Cory Gross

Almost 70 years before Steven Spielberg's *Jurassic* Park broke box-office records, *The Lost World* was unprecedented in Hollywood, featuring cutting-edge special effects that shocked audiences around the world. In this article Cory Gross (who runs the website *Sir Arthur Conan Doyle's The Lost World*) describes the film's inception and creation, as well as its legacy once the movie was released.

• • •

*"You forfeit your right to see the greatest entertainment the brains of man have ever achieved if you miss—*The Lost World.*"*

These brash words flickering across silent movie screens in the mid-Twenties heralded the arrival of one of the era's grandest films. *The Lost World* was the knockout science fiction, special effects spectacle of 1925.

The story of *The Lost World* on the silver screen begins not with that 1925 silent film produced by First National Pictures, but rather, with an unrealized version first developed by early film magnate William Selig, whose most well-known contributions to film were Roscoe "Fatty" Arbuckle and Los Angeles's first zoo. All that remains of the version of *The Lost World* that Selig intended to make is a synopsis, a scenario up to the end of the first reel, a potential cast list, and a handful of storyboards, all of which are housed within the archives of the Academy of Motion Picture Arts and Sciences. Selig's version was never made, as his company liquidated its assets in 1918.

Those assets fell into the hands of Watterson R. Rothacker. Their echo can be heard in the version that he ultimately made. It was Selig who first introduced the idea of adding a love interest to Sir Arthur Conan Doyle's seminal prehistoric adventure novel set in the exotic Mount Roraima region of Venezuela and Brazil. Several cast members on Selig's proposed list were eventually approached by Rothacker as well, including Lewis Stone as Lord John Roxton and Bull Montana as the Ape Man. Most implausible were the storyboards, which showed scenes of menacing saurian monstrosities, some of which look like they could have been drawn right from the finished film. The expertise to accomplish that feat lay with the discovery of Willis O'Brien.

Fresh from his string of stop-motion comedies for Thomas Edison and *The Ghost of Slumber Mountain*, Rothacker hired O'Brien to do the animation for this ambitious project. In those previous films, O'Brien's dinosaur models were built largely out of clay and cloth on wooden armatures. When hired to undertake animation work on *The Lost World*, he realized that what he had been doing up to that point was inadequate for a motion picture spectacular such as this. Furthermore, the sheer number of models required was too ambitious for him to accomplish alone.

The solution to this dilemma came in the person of a young grocery clerk and aspiring sculptor O'Brien met, named Marcel Delgado. For inspiration, Delgado went to the paintings of Charles R. Knight, the father of modern paleontological restoration who worked out of the American Museum of Natural History. By virtue of this relationship with

A still from the lost *Ghost of Slumber Mountain*

the paleontologists of his time, Knight's paintings were as accurate as science could make them at the time, and this worked its way into *The Lost World*. Delgado's models, 49 or 50 in total, were exact three-dimensional representations of Knight's paintings, and inherited their accuracy. The dinosaurs of *The Lost World* remain to this day the most accurate ever seen in a movie based on what science knew at the time.

The models Delgado crafted were carried by ball-and-socket dual armatures, upon which foam musculature and detailed latex skins were applied. Many of them included an air bladder for breathing effects. Numerous scale sets had to be built for the dinosaurs to stomp around in. Most ambitious was the massive 150 feet long plateau landscape used in the climactic dinosaur stampede sequence. Months upon months and years upon years of work went into every minute action that brought these ancient monsters to life on the screen. So convincing was the footage that Conan Doyle famously tricked the Society of

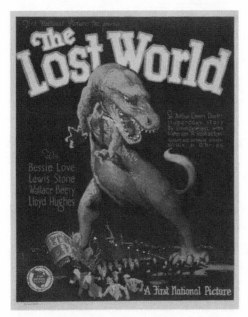

One of the most menacing silent-era posters

American Magicians into thinking it might be real when he brought a test reel to their annual meeting in 1922.

A cast for the Challenger Expedition were found in Wallace Beery as the irascible professor, Lloyd Hughes as reporter Ed Malone, Bessie Love as the love interest and daughter of the Lost World's discoverer, and Lewis Stone and Bull Montana. Animal actors found lucrative work in *The Lost World*, earning quite tidy salaries. If the rent paid on the animals was aggregated to a yearly salary, the python would have earned $36,500, Jocko the monkey would have earned $14,600, the alligators $14,900, and the sloth $15,000. Beery, Hughes and Stone were all insured by the producers against python bites, in anticipation of filming a scene that has since been lost.

Joining the main cast and the animals were, reportedly, an additional 2000 extras, 200 automobiles and six omnibuses for the grand finale in the streets of London. The London sets themselves sprawled an eighth of a mile, while the jungle scenes included a shallow pool that housed the sleepy Amazonian village and the crocodiles and alligators swimming beneath it. Principle filming was done on First National's patch of the Brunton Studios, a Hollywood establishment renting soundstages and space for smaller studios without their own property. Extra filming of the steaming waterways of the Amazon was done on the steaming waterways of Los Angeles' open sewer, which marked the border of MGM's studio in nearby Culver City.

Nevertheless, filming was completed after three years of tests and production. *The Lost World* ended up with a price-tag of $1 million compared to $200,000 or less for the average silent movie. Adjusting for inflation, *The Lost World* would now cost some $10.8 million (for comparison Steven Spielberg's *Jurassic Park* cost an estimated $63 million). Appropriately, the gala premiere was held at Sid Grauman's Million Dollar Theater in downtown Los

Angeles. Ten days later, *The Lost World* was reported breaking attendance records at the theatre. The film was both a critical and a box-office success. One florid review for the *Toronto Star* proclaimed "*The Lost World* returns in all its fantastic fabulosity of prodigiously unreal realism...This opus of Conan Doyle's out-Julesing Verne for improbability presented with all the veracity of a solemn melodrama is one of the most challenging pictures ever seen here."

Life intersected with art when *The Lost World* film helped promote explorations of the world's far-flung regions. The newly renovated New Gallery Theatre in London hosted a matinee performance in aid of the British Museum Fund for Exploration of South Africa on June 19th 1925. Sir Sidney Harmer preceded the showing with a lecture on W.E. Cutler's attempts to find fossil dinosaurs in the Tanganyika territory of East Africa. Today, Tanganyika is part of Tanzania, which is bordered by the Congo and the reputed home of a legendary 'dinosaur-like' animal named Mokele-mbembe. In its November 1930 issue, *National Geographic* recounted an expedition "Through Brazil to the Summit of Mount Roraima" and there were a few words spared to the doubtful possibility of finding dinosaurs upon it. An aerial expedition of the region was announced in *Popular Mechanics* a year later. Back in 1925, Katharine MacGregor—the first woman to cross the Andes from Peru to Paraguay—embarked on an expedition into Colombia to find a real life lost world. While MacGregor was heading to Colombia, Roy Chapman Andrews was preparing to depart for his second Mongolian expedition on behalf of the American Museum of Natural History. The first expedition, which got underway in 1922, had created a stir by the discovery of the first dinosaur eggs. The 1925 expedition, beginning in April, was expected to return more wonders. Adding to the furor over the whole thing, 1925 was also the year of the infamous Scopes Monkey Trial.

The Lost World received another important distinction—one of the first movies to be screened in an aeroplane. This historic showing was on Monday, April 6th, 1925 during a half-hour Imperial Airways flight from London to Paris. It was also shown the following day to a special party of 12 persons during an hour circle flight around Croydon, England. Not to be outdone, the German Air Service Company premiered the film on February 4th, 1926 during a flight over Berlin. The very first aeroplane in-flight movie had been shown as an exhibit during the 1921 Chicago Pageant of Progress. A Santa Maria hydroplane circled the Windy City as it showed the promotional film *Howdy Chicago!* which had also been produced by Watterson R. Rothacker.

Unfortunately, time was not kind to *The Lost World*. First National Pictures was bought up by Warner Brothers in 1929, who licenced the film to Kodascope Libraries, who in turn excised 30 minutes of dramatic footage from it. Clips were used in the 1931 film *Mystery of Life*, co-narrated by the Scopes Trial's Clarence Darrow. The whole film, and Willis O'Brien's career, was overshadowed by a certain 1933 film involving dinosaurs and a gigantic ape. At least the film inspired a boy named Bob Clampett, who drew upon that inspiration to create the beloved cartoon characters Beanie and Cecil. Now an inductee into the Library of Congress' National Film Registry, recent restorations making use of recovered footage have put some of the lustre back onto "the greatest entertainment the brains of man have ever achieved."

Cory Gross runs both "Sir Arthur Conan Doyle's The Lost World" and "Voyages Extraordinaires," dedicated to Victorian/Edwardian science fiction.
sirarthurconandoyleslostworld.blogspot.com
voyagesextraordinaires.blogspot.com

Various promotional stills from *The Lost World*

A Real-Life Cowboy:
William S. Hart and the St. Francis Dam Disaster
by E.J. Stephens

In 1928, 40 miles northwest of Los Angeles, the St. Francis Dam burst less than two years after its completion. Claiming more than 600 lives, it was one of the deadliest disasters in American history until that time. The saga of the dam has been told many times—but in this article, film historian and author E.J. Stephens tells a lesser-known story about the small impact made by one of the silent screen's biggest stars.

• • •

I download the directions and climb in the car. Soon, I find myself two miles north of Saugus, California peering to the west towards a clump of trees on the side of a barren hill. Squinting, I can just barely make out a white marker. This is the place. I follow a dirt driveway down into a dried-up creek bed. A "Do Not Enter" sign momentarily halts my progress, but since there is no place to turn around, I cautiously proceed on up the hill towards a house where my car is immediately surrounded by several breeds of barking dogs. I think better about staying and throw the car into reverse just as a friendly woman opens the front door and assures me that my life is in no danger. I tell her I'm there to see the Ruiz Cemetery.

"Are you a family member?" she asks.

"No," I say, surprised that there are still living Ruiz descendants after what happened in 1928. "I've just always wanted to see it," I add.

"Sure thing," she says, "it's just up the hill behind the house. And don't worry about the dogs. They'll just try to lick you to death."

I walk the couple of hundred yards back to the graveyard up a horse trail that leads through dried brush, always keeping a keen eye out for snakes.

The cemetery is about a half-acre square, with brush concealing many of the graves, and is surrounded by a weathered iron fence with a gate hanging precariously off of rusted hinges. It's a lonely place, but a sign by the gate with "Cemetery Ruiz" spelled out in turquoise reveals that someone has made it up here during the recent past.

The cemetery is dominated by the large granite Ruiz family monument in the southwest corner. In front of the monument are six smaller stones for individual members of the Ruiz family. From left to right they read:

Sister Susana B.
February 1, 1920—March 13, 1928
Brother Raymond C.
February 25, 1917—March 13, 1928
Brother Martin F.
October 10, 1908—March 13, 1928
Sister Mary S.
October 22, 1898—March 13, 1928
Mother Rosaria P.
August 15, 1875—March 13, 1928
Father Enrique R.
March 5, 1864—March 13, 1928

Off to the right are the graves of Rosarita A. Erratchuo and her infant son Roland. Rosarita was the oldest daughter of Enrique and Rosaria Ruiz. They both died on the same night as the rest of their family.

Even without knowing the history of this canyon, it would be obvious to the most casual of observer that something big went down the night of March 13, 1928. And big it was.

In the middle of the night just six miles up the road from the cemetery, the 180-foot high St. Francis Dam broke just hours after William Mulholland, the dam's chief engineer, had inspected it after hearing reports of leaks, and declared it safe.

The Ruizes and Erratchuoes were among the first of the estimated 450 victims who were crushed by the torrent of 12 billion gallons of water that flushed through the canyon that night.

I clear away some brush and find a memorial that reads, "In memory of those who lost their lives in the Santa Clara flood Mar. 13, 1928 / Erected by the Newhall Cowboys." I only know this from newspaper reports made in 1928. After eight decades, the elements have nearly eroded the lettering completely.

This stone was placed here by some real-life cowboys who worked the ranches in the area, and by William S. Hart—a man who played a cowboy on screen. Hart lived in nearby Newhall and was deeply troubled by the destruction that took place near his home. He took over the responsibility for the burial of a young boy whose body lay unclaimed, buying a tiny cowboy outfit for the child. The boy was going to be buried here, but shortly before his funeral he was identified, and was instead interred in Chatsworth near his mother, who also perished in the flood.

I climb back down the hill and pet the dogs on the way out. As I drive back through the wash, I try to imagine what it was like on that tragic night in the spring of 1928 when a wall of water eighteen-stories high thundered down this bone-dry canyon.

But my mind just can't do it.

E.J. Stephens is the author of Early Warner Bros. Studios, Early Poverty Row Studios, *and* Early Paramount Studios. *He has written extensively about the film history of the Santa Clarita Valley and was successful in placing a marker at the filming location of the last scene of Charlie Chaplin's* Modern Times. *E.J and his wife, Kimi, also offer tours of historic movie sites; for more information visit:*
http://newhallywoodtours.com

Letters from the Stars:
A Girl's Scrapbook of Mail from the Screen's First Idols

by Charles Epting

• • •

The scrapbook of Eloisa Mendonza reads like countless other scrapbooks created by young girls. Born just before the turn of the 20th century, Mendonza used this scrapbook to document her senior year at Battle Creek Central High School in 1915 and 1916. Its pages are filled with high school theater programs, graduation announcements, and notes from friends and family. There are dozens of ticket stubs, flyers, and newspaper clippings—the exact kinds of things you would expect a teenage girl to sentimentally hold onto.

Towards the end of Eloisa's scrapbook, however, one particular passion of hers quickly becomes apparent: she was a cinema fanatic. Not only are there theater playbills, tickets, and a newspaper article about the local screening of *Birth of a Nation*—there are about a dozen envelopes glued to the pages of the book, their original contents still intact. Mendonza didn't simply sit back and enjoy the films that came through Battle Creek; she actively wrote to her favorite actors and actresses, requesting signed pictures to add to her collection.

Collecting autographs was, at that time, very much a child's hobby. It would not be several decades until adults joined in on the craze, collecting signatures and creating a competitive market. In the 1910s, fan mail and autographs were simply the only way for a young girl from Michigan to feel connected to the larger-than-life figures she saw on the screen. The care with which the envelopes are mounted in the scrapbook is evidence of the reverence Eloisa had for these early movie stars.

The very concept of a "movie star" was still being defined when Eloisa was writing her letters to Los Angeles and New York. Before this time, many stars weren't even known by their names, but rather by the names of the studio for which they worked. Most notably Florence Lawrence was billed as the "Biograph Girl," amongst other monikers. Many audiences could recognize actresses like Lawrence and Mary Pickford, but because actors were largely uncredited they were known merely for their faces and nothing else.

The movie industry was in a period of transition in 1915. Heavyset funny-man John Bunny would pass away that year, paving the way for Roscoe Arbuckle. Before Douglas Fairbanks, King Baggot was the most famous leading man in motion pictures—a name all but forgotten today. D.W. Griffith's three-hour epic, *The Birth of a Nation*, revolutionized what a film could be—in terms of length, special effects, and countless other innovations. And a certain Brit with an ill-fitting suit and a toothbrush mustache was about to take the world by storm.

Mendonza's scrapbook captures the cinematic world at a critical time. The actors and actress who replied to her are not well-known today; it would be a decade before Greta Garbo, Louise Brooke, and Clara Bow were household names. Yet the letters she so delicately preserved preserve the true pioneers of Hollywood. In *The Juggernaut*, Earle Williams crashes a full-sized steam locomotive—12 years before Keaton would perform the same stunt in *The General*. Their relative anonymity today should not be misinterpreted as a lack of talent or relevance.

Instead, Eloisa's scrapbook should serve as a reminder that the "silent era" that is so fondly remembered today—the era of Keaton and Fairbanks and Bow—represents a mere fraction of the true depth of early cinema. Hopefully these letters, now a century old, rekindle an awareness for some of the world's first movie stars. They are reproduced in full here.

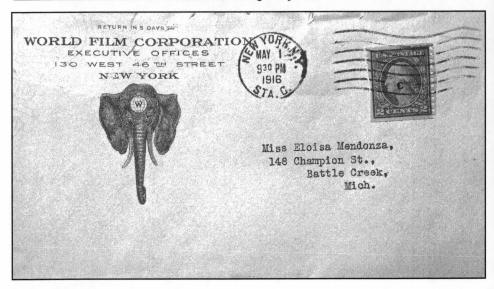

Dear Miss Mendonza,

Replying to yours of March 18th, I am taking the pleasure of mailing you, under separate cover, an autographed photograph of myself.

Trusting you will continue to like my screen productions and thanking you for your kind letter. I beg to remain

Faithfully yours,
Edwin August

Edwin August was part of D.W. Griffith's acting troupe, starring in shorts alongside Blanche Sweet and Mary Pickford. August was also a noted director during the 1910s and co-founded the very short-lived Eaco Films. Although he suffered a decline in prominence by the end of the decade, he continued to act in uncredited roles into the 1940s.

Dear Miss Mendonza,

I am glad to read that you like my work and I am sending you a photo under separate cover. May I ask you to let me know if you receive it.

Sincerely,
Edward Earle

Edward Earle was one of the most prominent actors to come out of the Edison Studios. With well over 400 acting credits to his name, Earle's prominence during the silent era continued all the way up to Lillian Gish's 1928 film *The Wind* and Buster Keaton's 1929 film *Spite Marriage*. He would later become a popular character actor in talkies and on television.

My dear Friend:

Your kind letter of recent date lies before me and your appreciation of my work well repays any effort I may have put forth in endeavoring to please the public.

It encourages me to hear that you understand and are in sympathy with my ideas of expression. In the future when acting before the camera I will bear in mind your praise and I am sure it will inspire me to do big things.

I am very anxious to have you see some of my latest pictures and am appending a selected list. Give them to your favorite Exhibitor and ask him to run the pictures. Particularly would like you to see "VENGEANCE IS MINE," my first five-reel release on the MUTUAL PROGRAM and the best thing I have done in years. In the future all of my pictures will be released in five reels on the MUTUAL PROGRAM.

Autographed photo has been mailed you under separate cover.

> *Best wishes of your good friend,*
> *Crane Wilbur*

In 1915, Crane Wilbur was best-known for his work in serials, including 1914's The Perils of Pauline. *Vengeance is Mine*, the film he promotes in his letter, proved to be one of his biggest successes as an actor. Wilbur went on to become a prolific director and screenwriter through the 1950s, with dozens of works including the campy Vincent Price classic *The Bat*.

Dear Miss Mendonza,

I have your charming note and thank you for the nice things you said. I take pleasure in sending you a photograph which I am mailing today.

> *Most sincerely,*
> *May Allison*

May Allison made her first screen appearance in Theda Bara's *A Fool There Was*, after which she began a successful string of pictures with Harold Lockwood. Allison and Lockwood were one of the first movie couples to be heavily publicized. After Lockwood's death in 1918, she made several more features until her retirement form the movie industry in 1927.

Dear Madam,

Your courteous letter received and in reply I wish to state that I would be more than pleased to mail you one of my photographs upon receipt of twenty-five cents in one or two cent stamps. I believe you can appreciate the number of like requests I receive daily, which makes a charge of this kind necessary to help cover part of the expense to me.

Thanking you for the interest, I am,
Sincerely yours,
Earle Williams

Although unknown today, Earle Williams was voted the top movie star in America in 1915. Paired with Anita Stewart, Williams served as the biggest draw for Vitagraph Studios. 1915's *The Juggernaut* was considered by many to be one of the greatest films ever made until that time. Although he maintained leading roles into the 1920s, his untimely death at 47 in 1927 caused him to fade into obscurity quickly.

Identical letters were received from Francis Ford and Grace Cunard:

MY DEAR FRIEND:-

Your letter received and I want to thank you for your very kind expressions.

I am very glad indeed that you like my work so well and hope you will continue to be one of my admirers.

I have placed your name on the mailing list and as soon as my photos are completed shall send you one. Wishing you a Merry Christmas and a very happy New Year, I am,

Yours sincerely,
Francis Ford/Grace Cunard

Although never as well-known as his younger brother John, Francis Ford was nevertheless a prolific actor and director. He was romantically linked to actress Grace Cunard, with whom he starred in Universal's first serial, *Lucille Love, Girl of Mystery*. Cunard went on to star in several more serials, and both continued to act in small roles for several decades.

Dear Friend,

I received your welcome letter requesting one of my photos, and it is with the greatest of pleasure that I enclose the same to you and hope it will meet with your personal satisfaction. From

Your true friend,
Unsigned [Charlie Chaplin]

Charlie Chaplin hardly needs a biographical introduction. When the letter was written on February 26, 1916, Chaplin was transitioning between Essany Films and Mutual Film Corporation. His first film for Mutual, *The Floorwalker*, would be released three months later. Although it is unsigned, it was written on Chaplin's personal letterhead while living in Downtown Los Angeles.

Dear Friend;
I beg to acknowledge with many thanks, the receipt of your very interesting letter and complying with your request I am enclosing one of my photographs.
Again thanking you for your interest and support to my screen efforts, I am
    Very sincerely yours,
    Edna Purviance

Perhaps the most notable signature in the lot belongs to Edna Purviance, longtime co-star and love interest of Charlie Chaplin. After making her debut in *A Night Out*, Purviance would go on to star in 33 films with the Little Tramp, including *The Kid*. After starring in *A Woman of Paris* and the unreleased *A Woman of the Sea*, Purviance retired from acting but remained on Chaplin's payroll until her death in 1958. She was included in bit parts in both *Monsieur Verdoux* and *Limelight*.

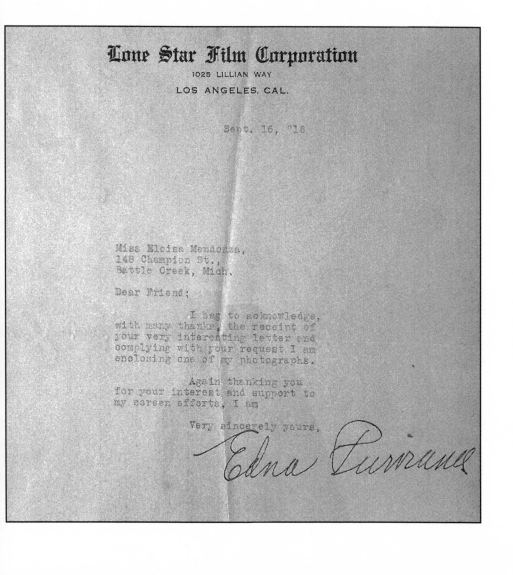

Funny Charlie Chaplin: He Could Only Make Me Cry!

Mrs. Charlie Chaplin, Suing for Divorce, Tells Sad Experiences

by Mildred Harris

In this rare interview from 1920, Mildred Harris shares lurid details about her brief marriage with Charlie Chaplin. Chaplin would repeatedly deny her accusations; 95 years later, it is still up to the reader to decide.

• • •

I am quite ready to admit that my marriage to Charlie Chaplin was a mistake. It was a mistake on his part, because he is a genius, and geniuses should not marry. He would be better free and remain free, for he will make any woman he marries miserable. I know.

We have been married for three years. For two years we lived under the same roof, more or less. That is, if greeting a husband after long disappearances might be said to be living under the same roof with him.

If lying awake, weeping and wondering where your husband is, until 4 or 5 o'clock in the morning can really be called living.

If wrangling over every bill that comes in can be called living.

If living on the scale of an income of $250 a week, when your husband earns $13,000 a week, can be called living.

If having your wardrobe censored and a standard of two or three dresses and one hat established may be considered an existence.

If being told to keep your head down so that no man will see your face is living.

If hearing that meat and potatoes and pudding are enough for a meal and that ice cream and salads are silly and useless really stands for proper living.

If being constantly accused of flirting by a man who is causelessly jealous is living.

All this and more I endured—and for twelve months. That is the reason I hesitate

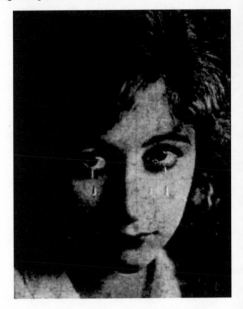

to say that we lived under the same roof. It wasn't living. It was perdition roofed.

It has been said that a comedian is only funny in public. I believe it. In fact, I know it. Charlie Chaplin, who has made millions laugh, only caused me tears.

So it was better that we should separate. Better that there be a divorce. I have seen him since my suit for divorce began. We met m the office of my lawyer in Los Angeles.

When we parted he said: "Mildred, you are right. I should never have married. I know it now. You probably will marry soon. If you do I hope you will be happy. I shall never marry again." And we looked at each other sadly—a funny man and his wife.

That the public may not be misled by strange, false rumors I will tell for once and finally, unless I tell it in the court, the story of the funny man who could only make his wife cry.

Mr. Chaplin and I met at the home of my aunt at the beach near Los Angeles. I was staying with my aunt. Mr. Chaplin and others were calling. At once he became attentive. We used to go for long walks on the beach. Ha talked about his life. He told me he was very lonely. He said he needed a home and someone to care for him. Older and wiser persons say that kind of talk is a prelude to a proposal. It was in this case. We "went together," as country folks say, for four months. We were married. We went to live in a big, lonely house on a high hill, Laughlin Hill, in Los Angeles.

At once began the woes of a funny man's wife—the reign of mental cruelty of which I complained when I brought my suit for divorce. Although I was married, the youth had not gone out of me with my acceptance of the wedding ring. I am not frivolous, but I am young. I like to dance and to be with people.

Mr. Chaplin didn't. He would never dance except to keep me from dancing with other men. He didn't like people at least, not people who love to laugh and sing and dance because they are glad they are alive. He brought men home to dinner.

But such men! Old, grave, and intellectual men! They were 50 years old or more. They talked of things I could not possibly understand. I was seventeen. What could I know of philosophy, or of Voltaire, or Rousseau, or Kant?

He liked to think he was a Socialist, though he didn't live like one. He wasn't willing to divide his money with anyone, not even his wife, as was invariably impressed upon me on bill day.

He thought my bills for dresses outrageous. He said, "You are married. You don't need expensive dresses. You have captured me. I am yours."

I used to reply: "But, my dear, I want pretty clothes to keep you. Marriage ought to be a winning over and over of the lord of our hearts."

He did not even listen. I had lost him again. I was always losing his attention. He is the most preoccupied man on earth. For this there is a good reason, I confess. He invents his own characters, and writes his sketches and acts them. That is the work of two or three men. Instead of staying at home with me, in our big, lonely house on

the hill, he left me cowering with fear, as a child cowers in the dark, afraid of nameless things, while he went forth to walk the streets at night.

He walked, as I have said, until 4 or 5 in the morning. He was looking for types, he was seeking characters and materials for his comedies. He seemed to forget I was in the world. I was not in his world of thought.

He used to leave home and visit our friends. He would be gone for days and weeks. He stayed with friends at Berkley Hills for two months. That was when I sued for divorce. During these absences there would not be a word from him. Then he would come back and resume the old gloomy life.

One thing that bored me was that he wanted to read deep books. Some time I shall grow into an understanding of them, but I haven't yet reached that stature. He would read those books to me by the hour, and would insist that I read them. Yet sometimes I found that Charlie fooled me. When I really read the books I read them. I delved into them.

And when I would talk to him about the plots and characters I found he had only a surface knowledge of them! My lord was guilty of skimming a book. There are literary poseurs. And yet Mr. Chaplin is ambitious. He wants to leave off the funny little walk and the baggy trousers and queer little mustache. Like all comedians, he wants to be serious. He longs to play tragedies. He used to rehearse tragic parts to me.

Fancy Charlie Chaplin as Hamlet! If the incongruity struck me and I laughed he flew into a fury and called me the essence of silliness. That essence of silliness is euphemism. You wouldn't print what he called me.

Although his life and thoughts were far from mine, yet he was madly jealous. His life had not been sheltered as mine was. In those days while he was growing up m Europe, he had not known the best women. He was surprised when I did not drink nor smoke cigarettes. He thought it a prudish pose. And he could not believe that the men whom I had known before I knew him were not my suitors. And it was impossible for him to believe that the men with whom I signed contracts or worked in the studios I regarded merely as cogs in the business wheel or professional associates.

While paying court to me and after our marriage he would say to me while we were in restaurants or were driving: "Keep your head down. I don't want any man to see your face." Or he would say, "Don't look at a man. He will think you want him." He had lived abroad too long to understand our open-eyed American candor. He even let jealousy enter his own studio. He watched me dance with an employee of his and said: "I'll fire that fellow in the morning."

Yet there would be recurrences of great tenderness. While I was ill in the hospital when our baby came he took a room next

Mildred Harris would go on to have a successful motion picture career before dying of pneumonia at the age of 42.

to mine. He came in to see me and bent his head over me and cried. He left me a note saying: "You are the dearest little mother in the world." Even the nurses said his thoughts of me were beautiful. But our baby died three days after it was born. His feeling toward me seemed to change. He grew indifferent to me. He went away collecting material. His room at the hospital was empty. He did not even call to take me from the hospital to our home.

I insisted on moving down from the big lonely house on the hill because I was afraid. We moved down to Oxford street. Because he left me alone so much I went back to work in the studios. And he was like a madman. We did not talk much to each other towards the last. We had little to say, because we could not agree upon vital themes.

I like domestic life. Mr. Chaplin is a Bohemian.

I like to make life as beautiful as I can. I believe in spending money to make it so. Yet when I told him that we could not be happy together and talked of a separation he offered me $25,000. This man, who is not as rich as the public thinks, but who is worth at least a million!

I want to be free from such dominion as his. I want liberty to do my work and have an uncensored home.

I don't want to be made to cry any more by a funny man—not even an American husband, who is one hundred per cent kind.

American men are 100 per cent husbands because they are good friends and comrades. Mr. Chaplin is a genius. He has been called the funniest man on earth. As a public entertainer he is above par. As a husband he is one-half per cent.

His ambition is like that of Doug and Mary. He wants to have $5,000,000 and travel. I shall be content with a modest living and a home. It is better that our ways parted and at a great distance.

Does Rudy Speak From the Beyond?

By Natacha Rambova

Just months after the death of her ex-husband Rudolph Valentino, *Photoplay* magazine interviewed Natacha Rambova, who was allegedly communicating with the recently-deceased Sheik through a spirit medium. Rambova was well-known throughout her life for her intense spiritualist beliefs, as can be seen in this interview. Her insights into the afterlife of the Latin Lover are presented in full below.

• • •

Is Valentino happy?

At first he was anything from happy. That was immediately after his passing. Three days after his passing I received his first message. Incoherent as it was, it showed Rudy as resentful and bitter at his taking at the height of his career. The spirit of his mother spoke, too, protesting at Rudy's terrible unhappiness. Then the tone of Rudy's message changed. Not, however, until after his final burial service in Hollywood. Concentrated public thought had held him earthbound. The prolonged cross-country funeral had held him in the agonies of the spirit in passing.

Rudy, of course, saw his funeral. He was torn with unhappiness as New York mobs fought for a view of his body. He realized his great popularity as he had never realized it and knew what he had lost by being taken. To him it was wonderful but cruel.

He was lonely, too. He could not reach his friends. He could not touch their sorrow. He tried to talk to them but they could not hear.

Of course, he felt the loss of adulation. Soon, however, the interests of the astral world began to hold him. Now he is radiantly happy, anxious to begin his work there.

Whom has he met?

He has named Wallie Reid, Barbara La Marr and little Olive Thomas. He has been most interested in meeting and talking with Enrico Caruso. Caruso, of course, was the idol of all young Italians. When Valentino first came to America, to make his living as best he could, Caruso was at the apex of his operatic career. To Rudy he represented all success and all greatness. You can imagine, then, his joy at meeting the great tenor over there. Caruso has taken Rudy to the opera and to hear astral concerts. Rudy, too, has met the personal friends with whom we used to communicate by means of automatic writing.

What have they said?

They have explained the astral world to him. He is slowly coming to comprehend the sublime qualities of the new life about him.

Does Valentino know of the sorrow that swept the world at his death?

Naturally, he was conscious of the world's sorrow. It was visible all about him. It tortured him in those earthbound days.

Valentino has referred to the opera and the spoken

drama on the other side. Can he tell more of this?

Opera and drama, sublime things of radiating tones, moods and colors, he says, are presented in massive theaters built of thought-substance.

Valentino has said there are no movies. Why?

Because the films are a mechanical perversion of the drama. In the astral world there is nothing mechanical. There is a point here I want to make clear. All inventions are created first in the astral plane. As earth-people perfect themselves and achieve the point where they can reach across, they snatch these inventions from the astral. Everything earthly is a materialization of something conceived in the astral plane. Motion pictures, on the other hand, require mechanism for presentation. Mechanism is material and consequently not of a part of the astral scheme of things.

The couple in life

What earthly successes does Valentino remember now?

He remembered all, at first. Rudy wandered the film theaters where his last film was being shown to sorrowing audiences. He walked his old haunts on Broadway, particularly around 47th street, where he used to spend many hours of his old penniless dancing days. He suffered because his old friends used to pass him by, unknowing. Yes, he tried to speak to them, without avail. He shouted "I am Rudolph Valentino" but they did not hear. It was hard for him to understand. He was just as alive, but in a different vibration. As Rudy has grown in astral knowledge, however, these earthly recollections have lost their appeal. The old glamour of the earth-people is passing. Our world is growing fainter.

Has Valentino any message for his old host of worshippers?

Yes. He has a message for everybody. He wants earth-people to know and realize that there is no death and no separation. He wants earth-people to miss his heartrending experience. He wants them to realize and believe in the beauty and perfection of this after-life.

If Valentino were to live again, would he try motion pictures?

He would try whatever circumstances permit. He would have to meet the problems of the earth-life.

• • •

Valentino, too, was a spiritualist during his own lifetime. In her later years, Natacha Rambova would continue to explore her spiritualist beliefs, even claiming she lived a past life in Ancient Egypt. She was published in the fields of healing and astrology, and even became something of an expert on comparative religions. Rambova suffered a fatal heart attack on June 5, 1966.

The Story of Greta Garbo
By Greta Garbo

On New Year's Eve, 1927, Greta Garbo sat down in a tea room in Santa Monica with reporter Ruth Biery. The notoriously reclusive actress proceeded to tell her entire life story, from her childhood in Sweden to her remarkable career in motion pictures. This story, originally published in three installments from April to June, 1928 in *Photoplay* magazine, has not since been reprinted.

Presented here, for the first time in almost 90 years, is Garbo in her own words.

• • •

CHAPTER I

I was born; I grew up; I have lived like every other person. Why must people talk about me? We all do the same things in ways that are just a little different. We go to school, we learn; we are bad at times; we are good at others. But we grow up, the one the same as the other. We find our life work and we do it. That's all there is to anyone's life story, isn't it?

I have been reading other life stories. Some people were born in red brick houses, others in plain white board ones. What is the difference? We were all born in houses. I will not have it printed that I was born in this house or that; that my mother was this or my father that. They were my mother and my father, just as yours were your mother and your father. To me that is what counts. Why should the world talk about them? I don't want the world to talk about my mother and father.

Nor my brother, nor my sister. My sister —she has died since I came to this country —I cannot believe it until I return to my home and find—she is not there to greet me.

My brother—he wants to come to America. I do not know. Pictures? He is so timid. But, then, I, too, was timid.

Why should I tell the world about them? They are mine! No, I am the youngest, but they have always treated me as the oldest. I can't remember being young, really young, like other children. I always had my opinions, but I never told my mind. No one ever seemed to think I was young.

My father died when I was fourteen. God, what a feeling. Someone you love is there, then he is not there. Gone where you can't see him, can't talk with him. You go to the studio, work all day, come home to the hotel, lie down, turn out the lights, and think about him.

The same flesh, the same blood—yet he is gone, never to return. Gone—my God, what a feeling.

I have always been moody. When I was just a little child, as early as I can remember, I have wanted to be alone. I detest crowds, don't like many people. I used to crawl into a corner and sit and think, think things over. When just a baby, I was always figuring, wondering what it was all about—just why we were living.

Children should be allowed to think when they please; should not be molested. 'Go and play now,' their mothers and fathers tell them. They shouldn't do that. Thinking means so much to even small children.

When I wasn't thinking, wasn't wondering what it was all about, this living; I was dreaming. Dreaming how I could become a player.

No, none of my people were on the stage. It was just born in me, I guess. Why, when I was just a little thing, I had some water colors. Just as other children have water colors. Only I drew pictures on myself, rather than on paper. I used to paint my lips, my cheeks, paint pictures on me. I thought that was the way actresses painted.

Long before I had been in a theater, I did this. I don't know where I got it; from pictures, from others talking—or just from me, the inside of me. I didn't play much. Except skating and skiing and throwing snowballs. I did most of my playing by thinking. I played a little with my brother and sister, pretending we were in shows. Like other children. But usually I did my own pretending. I was up and down. Very happy one moment, the next moment—there was nothing left for me.

Then I found a theater. I must have been six or seven. Two theaters, really. One was a cabaret; one a regular theater,—across from one another. And there was a back porch to both of them. A long plank on which the actors and actresses walked to get in the back door. I used to go there at seven o'clock in the evening, when they would be coming in, and wait until eight-thirty. Watch them come in; listen to them getting ready. The big back door was always open even in the coldest weather.

• • •

Listen to their voices doing their parts in the productions. Smell the grease paint! There is no smell in the world like the smell of the backyard of a theater. No smell that will mean as much to me—ever.

Why, last night, for the first time since I came to this city, I went to a theater. Went down to the Biltmore in Los Angeles. Went behind and talked with the girls; watched them make up; smelled the backyard of the theater just as I used to when I was little.

Night after night, I sat there dreaming. Dreaming when I would be inside—getting ready. I was alone. I don't like to be with people—and I can never stand any kind of fighting.

One night when I was going home, I saw two men fighting. They were drunk. I can't stand people who are drunk! One was big and the other little. The big man was hurting the little one. I went up and pulled on the big man's sleeve. Asked him why he was doing it. He looked down on me. I was eight years old—

'That's all right. You can go home now. Here's your little daughter.' Then ran away. I wasn't his little daughter.

It's just the same today. If I see an accident or hear two people quarreling, I am just sick all over. I never fight myself and I won't do any fighting in pictures.

I hated school. I hated the bonds they put on me. There were so many things outside. I liked history best. But I was afraid of the map—geography you call it. But I had to go to school like other children. The public school, just as you have in this country.

And I went to the movies, just like other children. I didn't see a regular theater—inside—until I was twelve. But I went to the movies often. I usually paid for my tickets, but sometimes, just sometimes, the man at the door could be persuaded to be kind, and money wasn't necessary.

• • •

And that's all I knew of the stage until I was sixteen. Then I met an actor. And I told him, just like millions tell actors, that I wanted to go on the stage. Asked him, just like all the others, how I could do it. He called upon another actor, better known, and sent me to him.

It was Franz Envall. He is dead now, but he has a daughter on the stage in Sweden. He said he would ask if they would let me try to get into the Dramatic School of the Royal Theater in Stockholm.

The School is a part of the Royal Theater of the King and Queen of Sweden. No, it doesn't cost anything to go there, but you are not paid for your work either.

You take a test to get in. There is a jury of about 20 people. Newspapermen—critics; theatrical people, actors, the heads of the School, and others.

I studied for six months. They gave me a Swedish play by Selma Lagerlov, and 'Madam Sans Gene,' a French one.

My test came on a beautiful day in August. It wasn't cold, but it wasn't hot either, as it is in this country. I remember it was right after noon. I was just seventeen. And I was frightened. My knees shook.

I trembled all over. Oh, I almost fainted afterwards!

I couldn't see a person. They were down in front. All I could see was that black pit—that black open space. All I could hear was whispering. I was so shy! I had never tried to act. The one-year pupils were on the stage. They read the lines of the parts which were not mine. I said my speech, all

right. Then I just ran off. I forgot to say good-bye. And I was so frightened. I thought they would think I had not been polite because I had forgotten. In a couple of days, they telephoned that I had been admitted.

Oh, God, I was happy! I almost died. Oh, now, even now, I can hardly breathe when I remember. For now, pretty soon, I knew I was to be a real actress!

But I was a very bad child. I upset the whole school. I liked to go out at night. We lived right in Stockholm and distances are not as far there, you know. You can take a taxi and be almost anywhere in five minutes. Any theater in the city. I liked to go to the theater in the evening.

• • •

So I was late almost every morning! Exercises came first—and I almost always missed them. The other pupils were charming, lovely girls who were always on time. Then, in would come Garbo, late as usual.

I'd come in the door and say, 'There's a rumor about that this school is still here. But I'm so tired; Garbo's so tired—'

And nobody would say a word to me!

Then it became serious. I started being late. If one had the privilege, you know. No, they didn't scold me. If I had been scolded, I'd have been there. I cannot stand to be scolded. Usually, we'd go out and drink coffee, all together, when I finally got there. Yes, they taught us dancing. But I can't dance. I was ashamed to dance. I was so big. Oh, yes, I was big. I was just the same size I am now when I was twelve years old. I haven't grown a bit since then. Isn't that lucky?

Everywhere I went as a child, I was pointed at because I was so big—so very big.

The school was wonderful. We had the very best teachers. We were given plays to study. Two pupils and a teacher would study together.

No, we were never on the stage. Oh, we were on the background of the Royal Theater.

We never said anything.

Just went on to learn what you call stage presence.

• • •

The usual course was two years. But I was just beginning the third, when one of the teachers came to me and said Mauritz Stiller wanted a girl to play in a picture for him. I said, 'Ya? I will go and see him!' I didn't think much about it. I never get thrilled about anything until it happens. It hurts too much to be disappointed.

That day, after school, I went up to his house to see him. I had never seen Mr. Stiller. To me he was just a very big man.

He is very big in Europe, you know; one of the biggest.

He was not at home. So I sat down and waited. Pretty soon he came in with his big dog.

I started trembling all over.

He seemed such a funny person. He looked at me, looked me up and down, looked me all over.

He has told me since, exactly what I had on, even to my shoes and stockings. I had on black, low-heeled low shoes, with black stockings. He just said a few words about the weather and things in general.

At times it seemed as though he looked away, but I know he was really looking at me every moment. After quite a few moments, he said,

'Well, can't you take off your coat and hat?'—just as though he had asked me a dozen times before, when he had said nothing about it.

• • •

Then just looked at me some more and said, 'What's your telephone number?'

Then I knew it was all over. 'He isn't interested,' I thought. 'When they're not interested they always ask your telephone number.' So I put on my hat and coat and went out. No, I wasn't worried. I just didn't think any more about it—

CHAPTER II

And a few days later, Mr. Stiller telephoned me to take a test at the studio of 'The Swedish Film Company.'

I was pleased, but not even yet, very excited. I do not get excited until I have something in my hand.

I went out on the street car to the studio with a girl named Mona Mortenson. She is here in America—in Hollywood—now. But she is going back to Sweden. The pictures are not so good to her. We went to the Dramatic school together. Was it not funny that we met on the way to take the test together and then meet again in this city?

The test was to me very funny. The stage is so different from the movies. On the stage you have your voice, but in the movies, only your face.

I was all shaky. I come off the street, go in and they make me up and then they take me in and tell me to lie in a bed and be sick. Very sick. I didn't know what it was all about. It seemed to me like a big joke, to come off the street and be right away sick.

And I was ashamed. I was ashamed to try and put myself over, as you say it. I had never done anything to put myself over before, and it made me very ashamed to do it.

Mr. Stiller waited a few moments, and then said, 'My God, can't you be sick? Don't you know what it is to be sick?'

Then I knew it wasn't play and it wasn't funny. I knew it was necessary in the movies and I became a very sick lady.

I went home. I still did not know whether I would get any part. I went on at school. Then, in a few days he called me and told me he had a place for me. I had it in my hands; now I could get a little excited.

And he gave me the part of *Countess Dohma* in 'Goesta Berling.' The very best part for my very first picture!"

The first days of work I was so scared that I *couldn't* work. I was sick in earnest.

Finally, everyone went out and left me. The electricians, the prop boys-even Mr. Stiller. He told me to practice alone. But I knew he was in some corner watching. I looked all around and could not see him, but I knew he was there. So I would not practice. I would not rehearse all by myself,—I would not look so stupid.

Lars Hansen played my leading man. Now he is back in Sweden—but there were no love scenes; not even a kiss. It was not an American picture.

The picture took a long time. There were snow scenes and we had to wait until it was winter. When it was over, I was no longer frightened. But I am always nervous and restless when I am making a picture. I cannot help it. That is why I never want people to see me while I am acting. I do not let people on the set. And I stay by myself all I can while I am making a picture. I sit in one corner alone, or go to my dressing room, or I walk outside by

myself while the others are working. I cannot stand it for someone to come up and say, 'What did you think of the football game?' as they do here in America. I cannot get back on the track. I cannot do my best work then. It is the same with every picture—I tremble always, all over.

• • •

When we had finished 'Goesta Berling,' there were no more pictures, so I went back to school. We have to make our pictures in the summer except for the snow scenes— No, school was not any different. I was still the naughty Garbo and still late in the morning.

When it came toward summer again, I had a telegram from Mr. Stiller. 'Do not make any plans for the summer,' he told me. Of course, there were other companies who might want me.

So I made no plans. I went away into the country. Oh, yes, I was alone. I always went away alone. That is what I like—to go away, far into the country, alone. An old couple to cook for you, look after your things for you. But there are not so many places in America where you can be alone. Here there are always the people—I miss it. Some people need to be with people. I need to be alone, always.

It is so wonderful alone in our country in the summer. In the midsummer you can read all night long, in the open. The little noises of the country, the wonderful air—Ah,—it gets you.

While I was there, I received a letter from Mr. Stiller. They wanted me to come to Berlin for the opening of 'Goesta Berling.' I went back to Stockholm and Mr. Stiller came for me—I have everything in the world to be grateful to Mr. Stiller. I have never seen a more beautiful inside of a person!

No, I had never been out of Stockholm except to my own country before. I was not so excited. I do not know—as I should tell this. People may not believe what I say—but I have the most amazing feeling,—I feel I have lived—before. I am never terribly surprised at anything. I feel always, I have been there before—that it is not entirely a new experience. I cannot describe—but I feel it.

• • •

Miss Lundequist, a very big Swedish actress, who played in the picture, went with us. She is a most marvelous person. She has the most amazing eyes of any person. So much soul and so tired, always.

Berlin was wonderful to us. Oh, yes, it was a very big opening. Everything that Mr. Stiller does in Europe is big. There, he is the master. Everybody goes to see his pictures.

We went on the stage. They sent us many flowers. They had sent way to Stockholm for us and they made it a very big time for us. The German people are wonderful. They do not touch you, yet they have their arms around you—always.

And Berlin! I will never forget when I came to it. The smell of the city. An amazing smell that has everything in it. You can feel it in your breast, when it is coming. I had not been in a big city before—where there were so many, many people. But I could feel the smell long before we were really inside the city—it was as though I had smelled it before—been there before, as I told you.

While we were there, that one week for the opening, people spoke to Mr. Stiller about our coming to America. He talked, but he did nothing. We went back to Stockholm, to get ready to make a German picture.

• • •

Ina month we went back to Berlin and then on to Constantinople, where we were to make the picture. There were to be many Turks in it.

Constantinople! I do not know how to describe it. It isn't like what people say about it. They are not in costume. They dress like European people. Except the very old Turks, who are dirty.

The streets—narrow with dirty little shops; dirty cafes filled with food which is oily. The lazy Turks—they are fascinating.

One day I was walking alone on the street and I followed along behind one of the old Turks; the dirty one with the funny pants. You know them? I do not know how many hours I followed him. He did not go anywhere; did not have anywhere to go but wander. He was so dirty, but so fascinating.

We never started on that picture. The company went broke. Mr. Stiller had to go back to Germany to see about the money which was not coming. I was alone in Constantinople. Oh, yes, Einar Hansen, the Swedish boy who was killed here in Hollywood not so long ago—was there, too. He was to play with me in the picture. But I did not see him often.

I was invited to the Swedish embassy. I went two times, but I did not like it. I did not want to be around people. I liked to be alone in Constantinople. I went to the bazaars. I had a guide with me. They are so big, you could never find your way out of them without someone to guide you.

I was so restless. It was a very big disappointment not to have the money for our picture. But I was not lonely. I walked around the old city by myself mostly.

• • •

I love to travel. I would like just to have enough money to travel. I have no place I want to go—except back to Sweden. I want to go every place! Back in the hills of China. To Japan. The Chinese and the Japanese have such strange faces. I wonder what must be on the inside of them. I would like to touch in China the little things that have been so many thousand years on earth. I would not care for company. It is not necessary to have company when you travel.

If I go back to Sweden, I do not know. One month, two—three. Perhaps it will be too small for me—I want to go everywhere and see every people.

Yes, I would like to go back to Constantinople. But I would not like to live there. The colors of that country. You cannot describe them. I would like to see them again, but not stay longer than the one month I was there then.

• • •

It was a shock, about not making that picture. But it was none of my fault. .Although I was so restless, why should I have worried? There were other companies and I was young—and was alone in a big, wonderful city.

Mr. Stiller came back and took me to Berlin and had me make another picture which he was not directing. It was 'The Street of Sorrow.' It was a very bad picture. When it ran in New York, the people did not like it.

Louis B. Mayer was in Berlin. He wanted to sign a contract with us for his company. Whatever Mr. Stiller said, I knew was always the best thing to do. I would say, 'Is it good?' and if he say, 'It is good,' I would do it.

When I met Mr. Mayer, he hardly looked at me. I guess he looked at me out of the corner of his eye, but I did not see him. All of the business was done with Mr. Stiller.

I signed a three year contract. The money was to be four hundred dollars a week and six hundred and seven hundred-fifty for forty weeks each year.

I do not really know what I got in Europe. That is the truth.

• • •

Mr. Stiller gave it to me. And it came and it went like all money. I am not a good business woman.

I went back to Stockholm to get ready.

It was strange; a very strange feeling. I was looking forward to something I had never seen. I did not know how it would turn out.

People here do not know what it means to my people when somebody goes to America. There is always much crying—a feeling that they will never come back to their own country and their own people. My people do not realize how short the world is. They do not know how the boats and the trains go. They feel they are going away forever.

My mother didn't say much. She said, 'I think you know better. I want you to go where you should.'

My mother and my sister and my brother went to the railroad station. My little mother stood there and looked at me. Her eyes were swollen—big.

My brother's name? My sister's? What does that matter? They are my people. Why should I tell their names to other people? Names do not matter. If I should read them—it would hurt. Hurt here.

• • •

I was very brave. All I said was, 'I will be back in one year. It is only twelve months.' I have been away two and one-half years.

My sister. I call her my little sister, but she was two years older. In only eight months after I had gone, she, one of my people, has passed.

That is the hardest. To be so far away when something happens. Your own flesh and blood—

I couldn't understand. She had always been so healthy. She was so beautiful. Then she got sick—just a little sick—then—

I would have brought her here by now. She would have been in pictures—

But the way things are here now. The way you have to work to get the results! Perhaps, it is better—my sister—

We sailed from Gutenberg. Oh, that was marvelous, on the ocean. I would love to do that trip over and over. You feel free on the ocean. There you are—and you cannot walk away.

Unless you want to walk on the water. It lifts a stone from you. You are almost—you are almost happy.

Happy is too big a word to use very often. It means so much to our country— the word happy, that we hardly speak of it. Here you use it so common.

I had a heavy coat on me and walked around on the deck and watched the ocean. I played that game where you push things back and forth, a little. I did not talk to anyone but a tiny boy. Little Tommy. I wanted so madly to give him cakes. But he had never eaten cakes. His mother and father were very careful.

• • •

Children don't get close to you. You can say intelligent things to children. When you talk silly things, they just look at you, and you feel they are thinking, 'Why are you saying such silly things for?' Children are very sensible persons.

We came into New York harbor in the night. When we saw the lights, lots of people screamed. They were from New York City. You felt it with them.

They felt like you will feel when you go back to Sweden.

I thought that America will be all flowers. I thought there would be almost carpets of

flowers on the streets of New York City. I wasn't terribly excited.

I do not get excited. But I was ready to see the flowers on the streets of the American cities.

CHAPTER III

No, I did not find flowers in New York City. I found heat! I came at a very bad time of the year. It was in July, 1925. I could not get my breath. We went to a very bad hotel in New York City. A Swedish man came over with us, who had stayed there before. I asked if all hotels in America were like this one. I was there three months. But I saw very little. I went from my room to my bathroom and back to my room again. I used almost all of the water in New York City. I stayed in the cold water to keep myself from being roasted.

I did go to 'The Follies' and to the Winter Garden. I liked that. It was fun to watch the American people.

We came to California in September. In New York, I spent all of my time in the bathtub thinking about how it would be when we got to California and I would start working in American pictures. Then it was four months here, before I started in one picture. I was to work with Mr. Stiller. When it could not be arranged, they put me in *The Torrent* with Mr. Monta Bell directing.

Yes, it was very different. The studio here is a bit of a factory. The studios here are so huge, they have to be kept as factories. Too many people in them to have it different. But I was a little afraid of them.

I could not speak any English. I did not know about the American people. In Europe we had always been working with just a few people. We knew everybody.

It was very funny. Before I had started on *The Torrent*, Mr. Mayer called me back into his office and wanted me to sign a new contract with him.

• • •

But I said, 'Meester Mayer'—I could not then talk but a little English and not so good pronunciation—'Meester Mayer, I haf not done yet one picture. Let us vait until I haf been in one pictures.' He wanted me to sign for five years with him. I could not understand it.

While I was making this picture, this *The Torrent*, and when I was finished, he called me into his office many times and asked me to sign for five years. I could never understand what he meant by it. We never said anything about money. He just said he couldn't afford to advertise my pictures and put money into me, if I would not sign for five years with them. I had already signed for three years, and why should I sign again when I had not yet a picture—and then when I had only *The Torrent*?

It was very hard work, but I did not mind that. I was at the studio every morning at seven o'clock and worked until six every evening. I was so tired. I did not go anywhere. I moved down to Santa Monica to be near the ocean.

I would go home and lie down and think, think about my sister and my brother and my mother, back home, in the snow in Sweden.

After *The Torrent*, I started on *The Temptress* with Mr. Stiller. But, Mr. Stiller is an artist. He does not understand about the American factories. He has always made his own pictures in Europe, where he is the master. In our country it is always the small studio. He does not understand the American Business. He could speak no English. So he was taken off the picture. It was given to Mr. Niblo.

How I was broken to pieces, nobody knows. I was so unhappy I did not think I could go on. I could not understand the English directions. Week in, week out from seven until six. Six months on the story. More than twenty costumes to try on over and over. That is why I do not care about clothes. There are so many clothes in every picture. I cannot think of them when I am away from a picture.

I never missed a day. I was never late to work.

It is not true that I have refused to work and have said, 'I will go home' as the papers have said about me.

When I had finished *The Temptress*, they gave me the script for *The Flesh and the Devil* to read. I did not like the story. I did not want to be a silly temptress. I cannot see any sense in getting dressed up and doing nothing but tempting men in pictures.

Mr. Mayer called me in and said I was to start right away. My sister had died while I was making *The Temptress*. My poor body wasn't able to carry on any longer. I was so tired, so sick, so heart-broken.

I went to Mr. Mayer and said, 'Meester Mayer, I am dead tired. I am sick. I cannot do another picture right away. And I am unhappy about this picture—'

And they said, 'That's just too bad. Go on and try on your clothes and get ready.'

'If people are not happy, I should think you would try and make them happy. I am sick,' was all that I answered.

I am not the kind of a girl who can powder my nose and say, 'Ah, go on with you.' What wouldn't I have given to have been born an American girl. To have understood the American language and the American business.

What could I do? I went to the hotel in Santa Monica and lay down to think. I did not think I could go on. I had heard of a manager. So I got one!—somebody who could talk the English language.

He saw how sick I was, how tired. 'Poor lady, why don't you go home and rest?' he told me.

So I went home for two days. Then I heard about the papers. They say, 'Greta Garbo go home'—'She is temperamental—she cannot be handled.' I did not understand that, so I went to my manager and said, 'Maybe I better go back to the studio. I have rested two days. It does not make any difference here whether I am tired and sick and have lost my sister. I do not understand and I will go back.'

So I went back and said nothing.

• • •

And there I met for the first time, except to nod to him, John Gilbert. And he was so terribly good to work with! He has such vitality, spirit, eagerness. Every morning at nine o'clock he would slip to work opposite me. He was so nice, that I felt better; felt a little closer to this strange America.

When I finished *The Flesh and the Devil*, they wanted me to do *Women Love Diamonds*. I could not do that story. Four or five bad pictures and there would be no more of me for the American people.

I did not know what to do. No one would tell me. I still could not speak good English. So I went to the hotel and sat down and waited. I did not know what else I could do. I wanted to be home in Sweden.

And the next morning they telephoned me to look at some sketches for the story. It was the first time I had not done what they wanted, except to sign a new contract when I already had a new one.

And I had a letter saying by not coming down to see the sketches I had refused to work and they could not pay me. What could I do?

Then a very kind friend told me about a man who would understand both me and the people of this country. I had a lawyer to manage me up to this time. But this new man, they said, knew all about the studio and all about the making of pictures. He had been in Europe a long time and would sympathize and understand that all I wanted was no trouble and just a chance to make good stories. So I went to see Mr. Harry Edington, and after talking to me every day, almost, for more than a week, and coming to believe that I was not all the papers had said about me, he said he would handle all of my things for me. My contracts, my money, my work,— everything. You do not know what that means to a girl who knows nothing about this big country and this big American studio business.

• • •

Since then, I have not had trouble. Because he understands both their business and understands me and my business.

But before I employed him I was home seven months without pay. I did not say anything or do anything. And the papers always said I want money.

I was terribly restless. I figured out that maybe the next moment I would be packing my trunks. I was so low, as you say, that I thought I would break. But it's like when you are in love. Suppose the man you love does something to hurt you. You think you will break it off; but you don't do it.

Finally, they call me and say they have a story. I read it and went out and asked what part I was to play and they said the little part. Aileen Pringle and Lew Cody were to play the big parts. Mr. Edington tell me to do it, so I did not say a word, but tried on the dresses and was all ready to play the little part in the picture, when Miss Pringle said she would not do it.

Then they called me and said I was impossible and could not be handled. For the first time I answered Mr. Mayer back. I said I had all my clothes fitted and was ready to play the little part. What more did they want? I am very sorry I answered back. I guess I did not understand them. It was all because I speak one language and they speak another. And the newspaper men who print all the bad stories, they could not understand either.

They said it was a new contract they wanted. So Mr. Edington fixed up a new contract, for five years. Because it was not money I had wanted in the first place, money was not so important. But Mr. Edington's contract did give me more money than when I came to this country. They had a cartoon of me in my country, holding out my hand with many American dollars. They thought I get five thousand dollars a week. That is funny.

Now Mr. Edington makes us understand one another and we are all very happy.

And that is all there is to my story. I am twenty-two years old and I have played in

• • •

I will go back to Sweden this year. I do

two pictures in Europe and five in this country. I was nineteen when I came to New York City.

not know whether I will bring my mother to this country. When I am working I like to be alone.

And if I were working hard—I love my mother. We will see.

I want to stay in this country. Hollywood is the place to make pictures. It is where there is a future for me or any other actress.

I cannot help it if I do not like to be with many people. I have some good friends. Mr. and Mrs. Jannings. Mrs. Jannings is a real woman.

She says what she means. Mr. Jannings is a real man.

I do not mean feminine and masculine, as you say it. I mean the inside, deep—real people. I have to keep learning German so I can talk with my good friends, the Jannings.

They wanted me to go to a Mayfair party. It was a nice party. But why do I have to go. I do not like parties.

I never know what I am going to do next, when I am not working. I walk on the beach for many miles. But I never know what time I will do it. I stand on the beach and watch the sea for an hour, perhaps two. What is that to people?

I like it. That is all there is to it.

I do not think one person should judge another. You can never tell why one person does not like another.

I do not think *one* person *can* talk about another. It is not of their own business they are talking.

I love my work. I want to be a big actress. That is natural. Do you not want to be big in what you are doing? And the other American people?

When I was starting *Anna Karenina*, the wardrobe department sent me flowers. I was so pleased. I know in a big factory-studio they cannot send you flowers and do things for others.

But—it made me feel a little closer.

Love? Of course, I have been in love. Love is the last and the first of a woman's education. How could you express love, if you have never felt it? You can imagine, but it is not like the feeling—who hasn't been in love? I am no different from the others.

Marriage? I have told many times, I do not know. I like to be alone; not always with some other person.

There are many things in your heart you can never tell to another person. They are you!

Your joys and sorrows—and you can never, never tell them. It is not right that you should tell them.

You cheapen yourself, the inside of yourself, when you tell them.

There is really nothing to my story, as I told in the beginning. I was born in a house, I grew up like other people. I have found my life work, and all I want is to do it and then travel.

I have had troubles the same as other persons. The company went broke in Constantinople, but I found another. Mr. Stiller had to go back to Europe. How I miss him. He talked in my own language. I owe everything to Mr. Stiller. I have not understood everything over here, but now everything is settled and we are all working together. I cannot stand trouble.

The future? I have no plans. After I go back to Sweden, then who knows? My contract is for five years, remember.

I have told the truth. That is everything there is to it. Honest! No, American cities are not covered with flowers, but I have found many flowers in America.

And that's all. My little story of my life in pictures,—of my whole life as far as that matters—is finished.

• • •

Garbo's haunting insights into her upbringing and family life help to shed light on the mysterious persona she would maintain throughout her life— particularly between her retirement during the 1940s and her death in 1990.

Original artwork for the articles was created by Chris Marie Meeker; it is reproduced here as it did in Photoplay.

Apostle of Pep:
An Interview with Eddie Cantor's Granddaughter, Amanda Gari

Eddie Cantor is remembered for many things: he was a Broadway star, renowned for his song and dance routine, interspersed with intentionally groan-worthy jokes. He was a film, radio, and television personality who delighted generations of fans with his trademark "Banjo Eyes." He co-wrote "Merrily We Roll Along," best known as the theme song for Warner Bros.' *Merrie Melodies* cartoons, in addition to coining the phrase "March of Dimes."

One aspect of his career that is often overshadowed by his countless other accomplishments, however, were the two silent films he made. 1926's *Kid Boots—* based on the Florenz Ziegfeld production that opened three years earlier—starred Eddie alongside the beautiful Billie Dove and Clara Bow, while 1927's *Special Delivery* also featured Jobyna Ralston and a pre-*Thin Man* William Powell.

Although his talkies (such as *Roman Scandals* and *Kid Millions*) are considered comic classics, his silent features have been

unfairly under-appreciated. *Silent Film Quarterly* spoke to Eddie Cantor's granddaughter, Amanda Gari (who is an accomplished actress and singer herself), about these two films.

• • •

It's interesting that Eddie Cantor received top billing over Clara Bow and Billie Dove in Kid Boots. *Can you speak to his stardom during the 1920s?*

Not being around during the '20's it's hard to calculate his appeal insofar as the era is concerned, but I do think great comedic timing is popular always. I do think that it was somewhat of an innocent era, and his "adorability" factor was off the charts. He could appear cuddly, but he also had an underlying sex appeal that came through. Mothers could love him, but he could still end up "getting the girl," even if she had to take charge!

Clara Bow was already a sex symbol when she made Kid Boots. *What do you think of the chemistry between the young starlet and the veteran Cantor?*

Women generally led Eddie in the movies, as his characters were often shy or awkward—"weaklings." With Clara in tow, what male would not want to be led? I am told by my mother that Clara actually told Eddie how to play to the camera. He was used to "playing to the balcony" which of

Amanda and Eddie.

course was not necessary in film. I think that friendship comes through, as well as her timeless beauty.

Eddie is known as much for his singing as anything. How do you think his persona translates into a silent medium?

I think Eddie was nearly equally expressive in his silent, because he had a terribly expressive face—first and foremost of course, the famous Banjo Eyes. But he was also a great physical comic, very lithe and energetic. Almost gymnastic.

Do you believe such a strong supporting cast in these movies helped to highlight Eddie's talents?

A strong supporting cast is always a plus —for any actor—but I believe his work could stand alone. Mostly because, although many of his movies had scripts that were less than stellar, his charisma and laugh out loud timing always shone through. But certainly Charlotte Greenwood, Joan Davis and Ethel Merman, amongst others, definitely rose to the occasion and played off his charms with great finesse.

Had his film career begun a few years earlier, do you think he could have achieved the same status as silent legends such as Lloyd, Keaton, or Chaplin?

I don't think that the timing of Eddie's movies affected his level of stardom in the movies. He was top box office for nearly a decade, (and did the same for stage and TV). What I think affected it, oddly, was the lack of remembrance in terms of the history books covering the times. Often, I think he was deleted due to the blackface material, which was indicative of the times, and no reflection of him as a person. I think he was easily as gifted a comedian as Lloyd and Keaton., and had the additional talent of being a song and dance man.

Chaplin, I believe, will always be in a class by himself because he was a writer and director as well as actor and a social commentator as such. He was also a dramatic actor as well as the comic who embodied The Little Tramp.

Amanda Gari has the distinction of having her birth announced by Cantor on the Ed Sullivan Show. More information about can be found on her website, www.amandagari.com.

Eddie Cantor and Clara Bow in *Kid Boots*.

Remembering Their Legacy: An Interview with Actor and Silent Film Historian, Jim Beaver

Jim Beaver is an actor's actor. Best known for his role as Whitney Ellsworth in the HBO series *Deadwood*, he also portrayed Bobby Singer on *Supernatural* and Sheriff Shelby Parlow on *Justified* (in addition to dozens of other film and television roles. In addition to being an actor, he is also a writer and director, having written and produced a number of his own plays.

Less well-known than his acting, though, is his role as film historian. While still a college student, Beaver published *John Garfield: His Life and Films*, and he has personally contributed plot synopses to more than 1,500 movies in IMDB (many of which are silents). *Silent Film Quarterly* recently spoke to Jim Beaver, a self-avowed silent film fan, about his personal favorite films and how he is influenced by silent actors.

• • •

Jim, do you remember the first silent film that you ever saw?

The first silent film I saw—hmm. It's funny, the first film of any kind I remember seeing was *The Silent World* [by Jacques Cousteau], which, despite the title, wasn't silent. The first actual silent I saw is lost in the fog of memory. The first one I can recall seeing was probably Chaplin's *The Gold Rush*, which I programmed for the Oklahoma Christian College film series I ran while in school. But I cannot imagine that I hadn't seen others before that. I'd been a film buff a very long time when I was programming that series.

How do the performances of silent actors influence you as an actor today, if at all?

Keaton is a big influence on me, as are Laurel & Hardy and Chaplin, though I don't get much chance to do out-and-out comedy. There are moments in the silent work of John Barrymore and Lon Chaney that surely have had echoes in my own work, and even William S. Hart has probably had an effect on my tough-guy parts, though one has to be careful with Hart! His sentimental side is a bit too

broad for today, though his tough side is still wonderfully effective.

To what do you attribute the enduring legacy of silent films—that is, why do people continue watching them more than 80 years later?

Those of us who watch silent films, who really enjoy and seek them out, are far too small a percentage of the population. But we're devoted, for several reasons. The best of the films, of course, were stunningly created, beautifully photographed, and the acting on par or better than much of the best today. Barrymore in *Beau Brummell* is as heartbreaking today as he was in the 1920s, and it has nothing to do with the times—it's just brilliant work. And silent comedy has no equal today. I don't mean today's comedies don't come up to the standards of the silents. I mean, it's an entirely different style of comedy. Fortunately, the silent comedies still work just as magnificently as they did when they were made, which I suspect will not be the case with many of today's comedies. But that's in part because what is funny in silent comedies is largely different from what is funny in modern comedies. The sight gag was once the linchpin of comedy. Today, the one-liner (or worse, the bathroom joke) is at the heart of most comedy. But because the silents comedies still work so well (in fact, more consistently than silent dramas), I think they will continue to engage new viewers, who will then be drawn into the full world of silent film. There will always be only a small portion of the population who "gets" silent film, but I think it will not be a diminishing small portion.

> ### Jim Beaver's Top 10 Silent Films
>
> 1. *City Lights* (1931)
> 2. *Intolerance* (1916)
> 3. *Pandora's Box* (1929)
> 4. *Sherlock Jr.* (1924)
> 5. *Steamboat Bill Jr.* (1928)
> 6. *Our Hospitality* (1923)
> 7. *Greed* (1924)
> 8. *The Wind* (1928)
> 9. *Napoleon* (1927)
> 10. *Sunrise* (1927)

Is there one little-known actor or actress from the silent era you wish more people could learn about and watch?

Well, for most people, *any* silent-era performer is "little-known." I wish more people knew about Keaton and Chaplin and Lillian Gish! I think people who know John Barrymore only from his sometimes hammy late-life sound performances would be astonished by the beauty and nuance of his work in silents. I can't think of a little-known silent actor who is little-known to *silent* film fans I would want to promote—most of us who are really into silents know *everybody*. I'll put in a word for Snitz Edwards, nonetheless. Pretty well known to silent fans, pretty unknown to everyone else. I just like him because few people that ugly got to have big film careers, and he should be appreciated for that, if nothing else!

If you could view one lost silent film, what would it be?

Probably most people answer this question with the uncut *Greed*. But if you mean truly lost, I'd have to go with *Humor Risk*, the Marx Brothers' first film. But I'd also love to find *The House Without a Key* and *The Chinese Parrot*, silent Charlie Chan pictures, and *Speakeasy* and *Words and Music*, with early John Wayne appearances.

In 2009 Jim Beaver released him memoir, Life's That Way, to critical acclaim. In addition to his role on Supernatural, *Beaver will star in the forthcoming Guillermo del Toro film,* Crimson Peak.

A still from Allin's 2014 film. "Home. Sweet Home"

Modern Mimes:
An Interview with Jason Allin, 'Little Tramp' Performer

Jason Allin—perhaps better known as "The Chaplin Guy"—is undoubtedly one of the leading performers of Charlie Chaplin's Little Tramp character today. A veteran actor and playwright, Allin wrote, produced, and starred in a one-man stage show titled "CHAPLIN: About Face." His online videos provide a unique modern spin on Chaplin's timeless character—in one, he depicts the Tramp dancing to Michael Jackson's "Wanna Be Startin' Somethin'" with a humorous effect. Allin regularly appears at film festivals, weddings, and other events in character, keeping the spirit of Chaplin's most beloved creation alive.

Silent Film Quarterly recently spoke with Jason Allin about his appreciation of Charlie Chaplin, as well as the unique challenges of depicting such a complex and idiosyncratic character.

• • •

Do you remember the first time you saw Chaplin on the screen?

I do not. I simply can't remember not knowing about Chaplin. More specifically "The Tramp" character. My earliest memories of watching Chaplin films was in the 70's when I was very young and seeing them come on TV from time to time.

If you could recommend one lesser-known Chaplin film to someone, what would it be?

I can't recommend just one or a few! Every one of them has some element in it that I want everyone to see. But ones that resonate with me the most slightly more than the rest are: *The Gold Rush*, *The Pawnshop*, and *One A.M.* Each of these held the richest information for me while studying Chaplin's movements and subtleties. Every film was vital for my studies, but these three drew me in more than the others.

What is the hardest part of Chaplin's persona for you to capture as a performer?

Tricky question; there are two personas that I needed to study to build my portrayal. Chaplin the man, and Chaplin's Tramp. I want to feel as though I am

Chaplin the man delivering my great discovery of The Tramp. I really need to study both. The tricky part is keeping things subtle and not over-acting with either personas. Many portrayals of either personas I've ever seen (Hollywood or not) have too much over-acting and assumptions that I just don't agree with. The first person I needed to impress with my portrayal was me. If I wasn't convinced I had something better to offer, I would't do it.

What do you think it is about Chaplin that makes him such an enduring figure in cinema?

I feel that cinema built up around the figure of Chaplin, not that Chaplin's figure stepped up in the ranks of the industry. Because of this, the longevity of his body of work is forever and timeless. The finer strokes of this brush are in the details of the character of The Tramp. He has mass appeal to the entire world to this day because of his design. He is one of us, he is the underdog, he is confident, he is flawed, he is personable. The Tramp plays with each and every one of us as he draws us into the story and situation with him by looking directly into the camera and communicating feelings to us with his face. It becomes a very personal adventure between the viewer and The Little Fellow.

The Tramp (Allin), grappling with modern technology

The Little Tramp character evolved greatly from its introduction in 1914 to its retirement in Modern Times. Is there a particular era of Chaplin that you specifically model your performance on?

Very hard to say exactly. My portrayal has become a hybrid mashup of Chaplin, the Tramp and Jason Allin. Because the Tramp is so recognizable around the world and etched in everyone's consciousness, the parameters are very narrow on how he is conveyed. That being said, I am still me and I am certainly not a replica of Chaplin. I approach my work as a role that I am doing as a job as an actor. I am not a fan is cosplay, but an actor in a self-imposed role. Because of this, I need to use what I have to work with. Age is a great limiter for me. I am 43 now and The Tramp is well known as the 25 to 30 year old Charles Chaplin portrayal. But the younger Tramp is extremely important for my body to know in order to become the whole delivery of him. My own mannerisms are ofter difficult to mask over and show up probably more glaring to me when I see my performance on film. This is a continued study for me and probably for any actor, but it will always be a work in progress. However, I will say my mind automatically goes to the very early rendition of the Tramp around 1916 and more specifically the look and movement in *The Pawnshop* but drifts to the 1925 version of him in *The Gold Rush*.

Lastly, do you have a favorite Charlie Chaplin scene?

When I let my mind go and allow a scene to pop in, I must say the part were The Tramp is assisting a customer with his clock in *The Pawnshop*. And the boot eating scene in *The Gold Rush*. The impression of these scenes are so strong in my psyche and I'm not sure why. Perhaps they may be the earliest images of the Tramp that I saw. I'm not sure, but I just adore them.

Jason Allin can be contacted on his website, [thechaplinguy.com.](thechaplinguy.com)

Manufactured by Amazon.ca
Bolton, ON

35175026R00037